The Positive
Power
of Negative
Thinking

The Positive Power of Negative Thinking

Using Defensive Pessimism
to Manage Anxiety
and Perform at Your Peak

JULIE K. NOREM

BASIC
BOOKS

A Member of the Perseus Books Group

Basic Books
A Member of the Perseus Books Group
Copyright © 2001 by Julie K. Norem

Published by Basic Books, a member of the Perseus Books Group.

Set in 11 point Bembo by Perseus Publishing Services

Library of Congress Cataloging-in-Publication Data

Norem, Julie K., 1960–
     The positive power of negative thinking : using "defensive pes-
simism" to manage anxiety and perform at your peak / Julie K. Norem.
          p.   cm.
     Includes bibliographical references and index.
     ISBN 0-465-05138-3 (hardcover)
     1. Success—Psychological aspects.   2. Pessimism.   I. Title.

BF637.S8 N65 2001
158.1—dc21   2001035481
                                                                        CIP

01 02 03 04 / 10 9 8 7 6 5 4 3 2 1

To my parents, Rosalie H. Norem,
Ken Norem, and Sandy Magnuson;
my husband, Jonathan Cheek;
and my children, Nathan and Haley

Therefore, since the world has still
Much good, but much less good than ill,
And while the sun and moon endure
Luck's a chance, but the trouble's sure
I'd face it as a wise man would
And train for ill and not for good.

—A. E. HOUSEMAN

Contents

1

Preamble to
a Contrarian View

In all affairs it's a healthy thing now and then to
hang a question mark on the things you have long
taken for granted.

—BERTRAND RUSSELL

*T*he positive power of *negative* thinking? That proposition
sounds almost heretical in American society, bastion of full
glasses, silver linings, and the ubiquitous yellow smiley face.
Can someone seriously argue that there are benefits to pessimism? That's exactly what I do in this book. *Defensive pessimism* is a strategy that can help anxious people harness their
anxiety so that it works for rather than against them.

Defensive pessimists expect the worst and spend lots of
time and energy mentally rehearsing, in vivid, daunting de-

tail, exactly how things might go wrong. Before a business presentation, they worry that PowerPoint might fail, that the microphone will go dead, that—worst of all—they will stare out at the audience and go blank. Before a dinner party they imagine that the new neighbors will clash with the old and the sushi will give everyone food poisoning.

Where's the power in this? Don't these negative imaginings leave us whimpering helplessly at the prospect of disaster? Why not be optimistic instead, look on the bright side, think positive thoughts, and give it our best shot? After all, research shows that for many people, optimism is related both to feeling better and trying harder.

Accentuating the positive is not bad advice, but it suffers from the same problem that plagues "one size fits all" clothing: People come in more than one size. Different people face different situations, encounter different obstacles, and have different personalities. Trying to squeeze everyone into an optimistic perspective can be both uncomfortable and unproductive, like struggling to stuff a queen-size body into petite-size pantyhose.

"RELAX—IT'LL ALL WORK OUT" simply isn't always true. We have to *make* things work for ourselves. Trying to adopt a positive outlook when we are anxious—an outlook that discounts our anxiety—can backfire. An anxious business person who denies or ignores her anxiety before a presentation actually *increases* the likelihood that she'll stutter, fumble, and lose her train of thought before a live audience; an anxious host who doesn't keep in mind the possibility of food poisoning may leave the fish out too long and wind up chauffeuring his guests to the hospital.

Defensive pessimism is a strategy that helps us to work through our anxious thoughts rather than denying them, so that we may achieve our goals. In this book we'll see how anxious people can turn their anxiety into productive motivation that helps them optimize their performance. Defensive pessimism is emphatically not about leading anxious people into depression; quite the contrary—it can actually aid our efforts toward self-discovery and enhance our personal growth.

I BEGAN STUDYING defensive pessimism back in the mid-1980s, when I was in graduate school. Research on the benefits of optimism was very "hot," and looking into the potential advantages of pessimistic perspectives automatically appealed to my contrarian side. Besides, à la *Rashomon,* I'd always been intrigued by the ways that people participating in the same conversation or witnessing the same event could have radically different experiences, which is just how it is with my married friends, Katherine and Bill, whose clashing strategies open the next chapter.

Preamble to a Contrarian View

Once I began to look, I found myself surrounded by people who were notably successful, by virtually any definition, and *not* notably optimistic. According to the research on optimism, this shouldn't be. Pessimism should produce negative results. When we set low expectations, we initiate a self-fulfilling prophecy. For example, if we convince ourselves that we'll never pass the test to get our driver's license, we won't spend time studying the manual and practicing how to parallel park. Once we get to the test, we'll have no idea how many feet we're supposed to be behind the car in front of us when it is foggy. Then sure enough, just as we expected, we won't pass the test.

But that discouraging description didn't fit all of the pessimists I saw around me. For example, my mentor at the time, a dynamic and successful woman who personified defensive pessimism (and who coined the term), utterly defied the prevailing wisdom that we have to be relentlessly positive to get ahead. Before every professional event in her life, she would regale me with an impressively impassioned and precise description of the failure and humiliation that awaited her ("So-and-so will be sure to ask about some arcane study that I've never heard of"; "I'll look like a little girl behind that huge lectern, and no one will take me seriously"), but somehow that failure never materialized. Instead, she always passed the test and achieved whatever she pursued; her career trajectory was and is straight up.

The Positive Power of Negative Thinking

There was plenty of research that indicated that people like her should be depressed, sickly, unmotivated, helpless, and hopeless—yet they certainly didn't seem that way to me. The researcher in me was driven to understand these people who apparently contradicted a well-established body of research. Why wasn't their pessimism debilitating? At first, I asked how these people were able to do so well *despite* their pessimism. Before long, however, I began to realize that they were doing so well *because* of their pessimism—and that's when things got really interesting. I began to understand that their pessimism wasn't just pessimism; it was something more. *Defensive* pessimism encompassed an entire process by which negative thinking transformed anxiety into action.

Since then, I have been gathering information about these people to demonstrate how defensive pessimism works as an adaptive strategy when we're anxious. I have run laboratory experiments that allowed me to take apart and tinker with people's strategies to figure out which parts do what and conducted more naturalistic field studies that measured the influence of strategies in real-life situations. I have interviewed dozens of people—both defensive pessimists and those who use other strategies—whose life stories add richness, depth, and complexity to the numbers generated by other research.

Throughout this book I use anecdotes from people I have interviewed (though I don't use their real names), as well as empirical research (my own and others') and observation to illustrate and animate these strategies. After eighteen years of research—years of testing hypotheses, watching and talking to people, trying to integrate results in numbers with the results from people-watching—I have a surprisingly optimistic story to tell about defensive pessimism. This story illustrates how anxious people crawl out from under their protective covers and face the world and their fears. It stars defensive pessimists, whose personalities reveal why their strategy fits them well and whose progress allows us to see how the strategy works; it features people who have developed alternative strategies, some of which work well and some of which do not.

I'll introduce Katherine and Daniel, defensive pessimists who have built satisfying and successful lives by confronting the dark side. We'll follow them as they anticipate disaster but, paradoxically, produce triumph in both professional and personal situations. Along the way, they'll tell us how learning to manage, rather than banish, their negative emotions has opened the way for ongoing personal growth and development of a clearer sense of who they are and who they can become.

Throughout the book, I'll assess both the costs and the benefits of defensive pessimism by comparing it to other strategies. Bill—who happens to be Katherine's husband and Daniel's business partner—is an optimist, and as we'll see, his optimism is also a strategy. It contrasts markedly with defensive pessimism and illustrates both the much-heralded benefits *and* the hidden costs of always looking for the silver lining.

Bill's strategic optimism works well for him, just as defensive pessimism works well for Katherine and Daniel. Both of these strategies can be effective, but we'll see that they are far from being easily interchangeable. We can't casually adopt another person's strategy and expect it to work for us, any more than we can put their shoes on and expect to be comfortable. To work, strategies need to fit the people who use them. Indeed, we may find blisters instead of bliss if we aren't careful to equip ourselves properly. Trying on the components of strategic optimism that work for Bill actually amplifies anxiety for Katherine and Daniel; similarly, if Bill tried to become a defensive pessimist, it could *create*, rather than forestall, anxiety for him.

However, some people may find that defensive pessimism fits *better* than their current strategies, if those strategies leave them floundering because of their anxiety. Our cast of characters will also include anxious types whose strategies don't stack up well against defensive pessimism, like Jeff, the avoider, who was the high school whiz kid, full of promise, but who is now confined to lonely, dead-end jobs because he's too afraid to try for more. And many of us will recognize ourselves in Mindy—the self-handicapper who copes with her anxiety by making sure she always has an excuse ready ("I couldn't find the files"; "I rushed to do it at the last minute"). She protects herself by never laying her best work on the line, but relying on her handicaps is ultimately costly. Her career and her relationships suffer because she cannot confront the world head-on.

For those of us who resemble Jeff and Mindy, defensive pessimism offers an alternative strategy for managing our anxiety and facing our fears. And although Bill's strategic optimism works for him, there are also optimists who have realized that their brand of optimism—especially if it is based on denial of the negative possibilities—isn't working for them. Too many times they have found themselves unprepared and off guard. They don't consider potential delays and are repeatedly late meeting their deadlines; a series of unanticipated disasters has left them shaken and shell-shocked. For each of these groups, learning how and why defensive pessimism works can pave the way for a strategy change that transforms victims into agents. I'll examine when changing strategies is a good idea, how to find a strategy that fits, and how to identify the obstacles to change and the routes to effective change.

I'VE BEEN WRITING this book in my head ever since my first research studies on defensive pessimism were published in psychology journals, but what finally convinced me to commit to actual paper was hearing the same reactions over and over whenever I talked about the strategy. Many who have never before heard anything positive about their own negative thinking respond with flashes of recognition as I describe defensive pessimism and palpable relief when I argue that it works.

People tell me that they feel vindicated when they learn that there is actually a name for their approach and evidence of its effectiveness. I remember especially the woman who rushed up to me after one talk and said, "I'm so glad my mother and my sisters were here with me! They've always worried so much about the way I am. Now I can just remind them that I'm a defensive pessimist and they don't have to keep trying to change me."

People who aren't defensive pessimists often remark that for the first time they understand what certain of their friends, families, or coworkers are doing, which makes it easier to tolerate. "I always thought I was supposed to try to cheer her up when she went on about things not working out," commented one surprised boyfriend. "But I have to admit that that got old pretty quickly—especially since she never responded very well when I tried. I guess I should just back off and let her work it through her way. I think that will actually be a relief to both of us."

Couples and coworkers who use different strategies also say that they are amazed at how often their disagreements or conflicts are related to those differences. A trio of nurses smiled as they described their ongoing struggles to cope with each other's strategies: "I'm clearly the defensive pessimist in the group, and they're always ganging up on me when I do all my negative stuff like worrying about whether the doses are right and nagging the doctors about their scrawls on patient charts," said one woman. "Maybe now they'll appreciate having me around more." The other two women laughed, and one remarked, "Well, I don't know about that, but at least now we can see that she's not trying to depress us on purpose." Having names for differences, and having a window on how one another's strategies work, helps to de-escalate conflict. Recognizing the sources of their frictions helps people to respond with humor and even, potentially, to appreciate the merits of others' approaches.

ONE OF THE MOST memorable experiences I've had while studying defensive pessimism occurred several years ago, when the research had just gotten off the ground, and I was a relative newcomer to the field. I was addressing a roomful of senior colleagues—of course everyone was senior to me then. I started by describing the results of several experiments that showed how defensive pessimism actually *helped* those who used it to perform well. Then I expanded on what I saw as the advantages of defensive pessimism—it helps us confront rather then deny our negative feelings, it transforms anxiety into a facilitating rather than debilitating emotion—and described people whose successes illustrated my points. Finally, and quite daringly, I thought, I critiqued the tendency I saw in the field to assume that positive thinking was always best for everyone.

Relieved defensive pessimists from the audience crowded around the podium at the end of the speech. I spent almost an hour answering questions, being regaled with stories, and eagerly copying down research ideas. After the crush slowly trickled away, I stepped down from the podium to find a well-established senior researcher waiting patiently to talk to me. With avuncular concern, he took me aside and gently explained that I had apparently fallen victim to a common syndrome among young researchers—the tendency to turn the faults of the people or process one is studying into virtues. He went on to assure me that—despite the evidence I'd presented, which had come from carefully designed experiments and been analyzed with appropriate statistical techniques—it was only a fluke that I'd managed to find successful defensive pessimists. Surely, he protested (as his concern transformed into irritation), I couldn't seriously think that there were advantages to pessimism, much less disadvantages to optimism?

In fact, I did think—and continue to think—just that. Lest I be accused of exaggerating its virtues, however, I should

Preamble to a Contrarian View

make clear from the outset that I *don't* think defensive pessimism is the ultimate solution to the world's problems, or even to the problems of any particular couple or individual. Defensive pessimists are neither saints nor paragons, and defensive pessimism has both costs and benefits. People are different, and what works well for some people may not work well for others—that's the point. (And what works well in some situations may not work well in all situations.) The costs and benefits of any strategy depend on who is using the strategy and what the circumstances are.

My senior colleague's comment obviously didn't convince me that I was wrong in trying to identify the merits of defensive pessimism. It did, however, illustrate for me how difficult it can be for people who have embraced the power of positive thinking to accept those merits. That's a lesson I relearn almost daily—and it continues to surprise me. We at least pay lip service to the advantages of racial, ethnic, religious, and gender diversity, but we have enormous difficulty recognizing the legitimacy—and potential advantages—of personality differences.

Most people in American culture strongly believe in the power of positive thinking. Within my field, "positive psychology" is a movement that's become a juggernaut, barreling into the public eye via newspapers, magazines, books, and the Internet. Its influence generally reinforces popular belief, even though the leaders of positive psychology actually promote a message that is more textured and more extensive than "look on the bright side" or "think positively." I'll be examining that message more specifically as I contrast defensive pessimism with positive thinking strategies and I review what the research tells us about the potential pitfalls of different strategies.

Precisely because the positivity zeitgeist is so strong and compelling, we need to work to reframe the oversimplified picture that equates optimism with all that is good and pessimism with all that is evil. Addressing the positive power of negative thinking will expose, and encourage us to explore, some of the assumptions we make about positive thinking—and even some of the costs of optimism, which we may underestimate or fail to notice.

Arguing for the benefits of negative thinking is contrary only to the assumption that optimism is an unadulterated virtue. It is not contrary to the aims of positive psychology, which include understanding how people can realize their full potential. Indeed, *negative* thinking is *positive* psychology when it helps, as defensive pessimism does, people achieve their goals.

2

Accentuating the Negative

A STRATEGY, NOT A SYMPTOM

Pessimists have only pleasant surprises . . .

—NERO WOLFE

THE DEFENSIVE PESSIMIST

Katherine is a successful sociology professor at an elite university. She's bright, she works hard, and she's enthusiastic about her work. You might be surprised to discover that Katherine is also often pessimistic. When she's planning a research project, putting together a panel of speakers for a campus event, or even arranging a colleague's retirement dinner, she's convinced that everything will be a disaster. She obsesses about every detail and agonizes about all the things that could go wrong. Of course, all of us who know her are quite confident that everything will turn out well: The research will be illuminating, the speakers will be interesting, the dinner will be a glorious success—and the vast majority of the time, we're right.

Katherine is married to Bill.

THE STRATEGIC OPTIMIST

Bill is a partner in a successful architectural firm and an upbeat, cheerful guy. Bill is quite popular both at work and in his social circle; he radiates energy, and people respond well to his obvious self-confidence and good humor. Bill rarely hesitates before agreeing to a new endeavor, and he is uniformly encouraging to those who approach him with ideas they would like to pursue. He has no patience, however, for naysayers. When his wife questions whether they can really get twelve errands done before they have to get to the airport to catch their flight, he rolls his eyes. When his partner, Daniel, brings up potential problems as they prepare for a presentation to a client, he laughs, first in mock exasperation, and then—if Daniel persists—with real irritation. Before their presentation, Bill will distract himself by answering e-mails or relax by browsing through travel brochures.

COMPARING STRATEGIES

Katherine and Bill are similar in many ways: Both are intelligent and highly educated; they both have good jobs and a network of caring friends and family. Clinical psychologists would describe them as "high-functioning," which means that they get through the day without major disruptions from whatever psychological "issues" they may have. They pretty much get done what needs to be done—and, importantly, they also get done most of what they *want* to get done.

They are strikingly different, however, in at least one respect: They take very different approaches to pursuing the goals that are important to them. Specifically, they use very different strategies for dealing with the anxiety that can derail their attempts to accomplish what they want to do. Their approaches are so different that each has difficulty understanding how the other's strategy can make sense.

Katherine uses defensive pessimism. She sets low expectations for upcoming situations or events and then reviews all the outcomes she can imagine. She spends a lot of time and energy mentally rehearsing or "playing through" the possibilities until she has a clear idea of everything she needs to do in order to have the best shot at success.

Why does Katherine, time after time, continue to be pessimistic and continue to reflect endlessly on all the things that might go wrong? Why does she put herself and those around her through all the extra agony and hassle rather than simply recognizing that things have gone well in the past, they are likely to go well in the future, and all this fuss and worry is unnecessary?

The answer is that Katherine continues to use defensive pessimism because it works for her in empowering ways. Katherine is anxious about things like publishing her research, taking responsibility for public events, and making sure that special occasions are special enough. She knows that the past can't guarantee the future, so she takes control of both her own anxiety and the situations she's in charge of by focusing on the potential downside when she prepares for upcoming events. She spends time mulling over whether aging Professor Smith will be able to hear if she puts him at the middle table for the retirement dinner, whether Professor Jones can be trusted not to tell off-color jokes if she lets him give a toast, and whether her retiring colleague's quarreling students will be able to sit at the same table without obvious hostility during the festivities. She can't control their behavior completely, but rather than simply worry about it all through the dinner, she will do her best to anticipate, and then fend off, the disasters that she can foresee.

Other people often find her negativity off-putting, at least until they understand its function. Her husband, Bill, sometimes feels as if Katherine is being negative "on purpose"—for no reason other than to be irritating. But it's not like that at all. Katherine is an anxious person—she would feel right at home in a Woody Allen movie. Defensive pessimism is the way she manages her anxiety so that it doesn't keep her from doing what she wants to do.

WHEN BILL SEES how people like Katherine or his business partner, Daniel (who, perhaps not coincidentally, is also a defensive pessimist), go about their work—their lives—he simply doesn't understand what all the fuss is about. For Bill and those like him, the best course of action is simply to do what needs to be done without a lot of reflection and without angst. Bill would never describe himself as anxious or pessimistic. Indeed, the closest he might get is to say that all the rumination Katherine and Daniel insist upon before any important event makes him feel "restless" and that he'd much rather just "get on with it." When things go wrong for Bill, his typical reaction is to shrug philosophically, extract whatever consolation he can, and look ahead to the next endeavor. When things go well, he congratulates himself and celebrates his success with those around him.

Bill engages in what I call "strategic optimism": He sets high expectations before an important situation or event and then actively avoids dwelling on how things will go. He works hard and is generally well prepared, but his preparation does not stem from mental rehearsal ahead of time. In fact, he seeks out distractions that help him avoid that kind of rehearsal.

Bill's problem is not that he needs to cope with anxiety as he anticipates upcoming events; instead, he needs to avoid arousing anxiety in the first place. He feels edgy when his partner insists on playing through every contingency because that just creates anxiety that he wouldn't feel otherwise. Bill distracts himself not from actual anxiety but from *potential* anxiety. When he sits back in his chair to read travel brochures, he's already confident that he's done what's necessary for things to go well. For him, further reflection serves no positive purpose.

AT FIRST GLANCE, it might seem that Bill's strategic optimism is preferable to Katherine's defensive pessimism and that any responsible author ought to be devoting pages to explaining how to adopt that strategy, rather than touting the benefits of negative thinking. And, indeed, there are many psychologists who would agree with that judgment and who "prescribe" optimism for those who are looking to change their outlook on life. Almost any bookstore or library will have plenty of volumes in the self-help section on how to become more optimistic.

But prescribing optimism for everyone misses a fundamental point. Bill and Katherine are using different strategies because they have to meet different challenges; they have different subjective or internal problems. Their situations are not different because of the different content of their jobs; their situations are different because of the different content of their psyches.

Simply put, Bill does not typically feel anxious, but Katherine does. She needs a strategy to effectively manage her anxiety, and he needs one that helps him to stay anxiety-free. As we compare strategies, we need to be careful to take into account the psychological situations that those strategies address—and our anxiety (or lack thereof) plays a powerful role in constructing those psychological situations. Strategic optimism offers no way for Katherine to handle her anxiety, and without such a tool, she is vulnerable to all of the potential disruptions anxiety can cause (as we will see in the next chapter). Only after we make sense of the problems to be solved—of Katherine's unique psychological situation—can we adequately compare different solutions.

Strategies, from that perspective, can be understood as tools designed for particular tasks. Bill's strategic optimism is an admirable tool that works well to motivate him and to help prevent him from developing anxiety, just as a hammer works very well for pounding in nails. Strategic optimism, however, does not work for all situations any more than a hammer works for all tasks in carpentry. It makes just about as much sense to recommend strategic optimism to someone who is anxious as it does to offer a hammer to someone who needs to screw in a bolt.

It does make sense to evaluate the efficacy of different tools designed for the same job and, based on the results, to recommend the best tool for a particular task. If the psychological task is to manage anxiety so that it not only won't interfere with performance but can actually be harnessed to enhance it, then Katherine's defensive pessimism starts to look like a pretty positive form of negative thinking.

VARIETIES OF PESSIMISM AND OPTIMISM

Psychologists also use different tools in their attempts to describe and understand how people function. The terms optimism and pessimism, in addition to their meanings in everyday use, describe several distinct concepts in psychology. Unfortunately, we don't all work with the same concepts, yet we draw on many of the same words to describe the phenomena we study. Different researchers, with slightly different aims and perspectives, focus on somewhat different processes. Psychologists working to disseminate their research to the public often adopt the shorthand of "optimism" and "pessimism" to refer to concepts that are different from what nonresearchers mean by those terms. From the outset, then, it is important that we distinguish defensive pessimism and strategic optimism from some of the other kinds of optimism and pessimism out there, starting with a look at the most basic and general kind.

Dispositions and Strategies

Some people, "Pollyanna" types, always expect the best in every situation. Others—"nattering nabobs of negativism," in Spiro Agnew's memorable phrase—are grimly convinced that disaster lurks around every corner. The terms *dispositional optimism* and *dispositional pessimism* describe those stable tendencies toward either positive or negative expectations.

The term disposition conveys that a characteristic is likely to influence behavior across a variety of situations and is relatively unlikely to change much over time. Dispositionally optimistic children usually grow up to be optimistic adults, and throughout their lives they tend to have positive expectations about relationships, work, recreation—most all of their endeavors. Often there is some genetic influence on our dispositions, and indeed, there is evidence to suggest that genes play a role in the development of dispositional optimism and pessimism (though exactly how big a role is not yet clear). However, whatever genetic influence exists is played out through interactions with the environment; there is no direct relationship between a particular gene and an optimistic or pessimistic disposition.

Accentuating the Negative

Dispositional optimism and pessimism are the psychological constructs that most resemble how we use optimism and pessimism in everyday language. When we casually describe people as optimists ("she sees the glass as half full") or pessimists ("his glass is always half empty"), we don't necessarily mean that they are as extreme as Pollyanna or the Grinch, but we usually do mean that their characteristic expectations are *either* positive or negative. Most people assume that optimism and pessimism are the opposite ends of the same dimension, implying that the more optimistic you are, the less pessimistic you are, and vice versa.

But people turn out to be complex in ways we don't notice through casual observation. Sometimes the same person will have *both* positive and negative characteristics: We may expect to win the lottery at the same time that we expect to lose our job. And some people may be hard to describe as *either* optimistic or pessimistic—they don't seem to have a single, definable outlook or expectation about the future. Thus, it turns out that optimism and pessimism, rather than being opposite ends of the same scale, constitute their own distinct dimensions.

In other words, people may be high in optimism (or medium or low), but that doesn't necessarily mean that they are low (or medium or high) in pessimism. Someone who will mortgage the house to act on a hot stock tip may also believe that she will never meet the right guy. The two dimensions are correlated, but they are not flip sides of the same thing. Some people are both strongly optimistic *and* strongly pessimistic ("I'll be brilliant; they'll think I'm an idiot"); others are neither particularly one nor particularly the other. And then there are all the permutations in between.

Relatively few people care about whether optimism and pessimism are one dimension or two, but it makes a difference when it comes to understanding the implications of research in our lives. Regular old optimism, for example, has received a lot of credit for its relationship with better physical health, which might lead us to call for clinical interventions that increase optimism in patients. Yet, in keeping with the principle of separate dimensions, it may not be the presence of optimism so much as the absence of dispositional pessimism that is important to those reported health benefits—and at least one study has found that to be the case. In that study, despite predictions, optimism itself wasn't related to blood pressure overall, and when optimists were in a bad mood, their blood pressure was just as high as anyone else's. It was the level of *pessimism* that was specifically related to chronic blood pressure levels (more pessimism was related to higher ambulatory blood pressure). If that's the case, then increasing optimism would be less effective than reducing pessimism.

There's a chasm between dispositional and strategic optimism and between dispositional and defensive pessimism, however. Although defensive pessimists are more pessimistic and less optimistic overall than strategic optimists, they are by no means pessimistic all the time or in every situation. Katherine, for instance, is firmly optimistic about her relationships with other people and the world in general—and she even secretly believes that she'll win the Irish Sweepstakes someday; her pessimism comes out only in specific contexts where her anxiety is acute. Bill—our prototypical strategic optimist—isn't optimistic across the board either; he thinks negatively about money matters, for one thing, as well as about many situations in which his daughter (who is just starting to date) is involved.

When we look across different situations in people's lives, we see that strategies, unlike dispositions, may be applied discriminatingly. Katherine isn't anxious about money (despite the fact that Bill is and despite his efforts to get her to take it more seriously), and consequently, she doesn't need to rely on defensive pessimism when she deals with money matters. Our dispositions are very general, and they influence our overall outlook; our characteristic strategies may surface only in reaction to particular situations or goals.

Attributional Styles and Strategies

Researchers have also used optimism and pessimism almost as nicknames for much more complex constructs. Several popular books and scores of journal articles address the ways people ordinarily explain the positive and negative things that happen to them. Our explanations are called attributions, and our typical patterns of attributions may be optimistic or pessimistic because of the way they reflect our interpretations of the past and influence our expectations about the future.

Strategic optimists do have an optimistic attributional style, but defensive pessimists do not have the typical pessimistic style. Katherine would never conclude—as those with a pessimistic attributional style would be apt to do—that because students fell asleep or looked confused during one of her lectures, she doesn't have what it takes to be a good teacher. Instead, she would scrounge around for livelier examples and get advice on her use of visual aids, so that the next time she gave that lecture she had done everything possible to make it both captivating and instructive.

Defensive pessimists make attributions, but they don't fit into the stylistic categories of optimistic and pessimistic—their attributions are different from both of those styles. Strategies in general are also different from attributional styles, because they refer to how we *prepare* for situations, rather than how we explain them after the fact. Although Katherine has a reputation for being obsessive, defensive pessimism doesn't lead her to ruminate on what has already happened; she may draw on past experiences as she prepares for new situations (conjuring up a vivid image of snoring students to spur her preparation for the next semester), but her energies are devoted to the future.

Positive Illusions

The terms *positive thinking* and *positive illusions* refer to a collection of processes that are also sometimes lumped together under the heading of optimism. These illusions—mild distortions of reality—sometimes help people maintain a positive sense of self and a feeling of control over their lives. We may selectively remember the good things people say, for example, and "forget" the negative ones, or convince ourselves that our successes are much more indicative of our ability than our failures. Studies show, for example, that when nondepressed people play a video game and are told they've done poorly, they tend to deny having had control over their low scores; however, if they are told they've done well, they claim that their skill produced their high scores.

These same people often unrealistically underestimate their personal risk of developing a serious illness or being involved in accidents during their lifetime, and they are likely to overestimate their personal contributions to group endeavors. They believe that even though they smoke, they are unlikely to develop lung cancer, and even though there was an eight-person committee organizing the charity dance, it was primarily their own catalytic efforts that pulled in record donations. Those conclusions reflect a positive bias toward ourselves that can be motivating as well as self-protective.

Strategic optimists tend to indulge in these positive illusions, and defensive pessimists don't—with important consequences for their self-concepts and relationships with others. Bill, for instance, assumes that when his client rejects his plans for her new townhouse, her decision reflects her bad taste rather than his failure to design something appropriate for her; her evaluation of his work doesn't lower his self-evaluation—just his opinion of her. But again, both defensive pessimism and strategic optimism involve more than just the presence or absence of these illusions.

MEASURING DEFENSIVE PESSIMISM AND STRATEGIC OPTIMISM

One of the ways to get a feel for defensive pessimism is to look at how it is measured for research. Below is a modified version of the questionnaire I use to identify people who typically use defensive pessimism and strategic optimism. The questions illustrate some of the ways in which defensive pessimism and strategic optimism are different from some of the other concepts I've just reviewed.

In our research, we select participants at the extreme ends of this scale to magnify the contrast between the groups. In reality, of course, most of us are composites of multiple strategies, and this questionnaire assesses only the extent to which someone is *either* a defensive pessimist *or* a strategic optimist in the *particular* situation one is thinking about when rating these statements.

DEFENSIVE PESSIMISM QUESTIONNAIRE

Think of a situation where you want to do your best. It may be related to work, to your social life, or to any of your goals. When you answer the following questions, please think about how you prepare for that kind of situation. Rate how true each statement is for you.

1 2 3 4 5 6 7

Not at all true of me   *Very true of me*

____ I often start out expecting the worst, even though I will probably do OK.

____ I worry about how things will turn out.

____ I carefully consider all possible outcomes.

____ I often worry that I won't be able to carry through my intentions.

____ I spend lots of time imagining what could go wrong.

_____ I imagine how I would feel if things went badly.

_____ I try to picture how I could fix things if something went wrong.

_____ I'm careful not to become overconfident in these situations.

_____ I spend a lot of time planning when one of these situations is coming up.

_____ I imagine how I would feel if things went well.

_____ In these situations, sometimes I worry more about looking like a fool than doing really well.

_____ Considering what can go wrong helps me to prepare.

To figure out where you stand, add your scores for all the questions. Possible scores range from 12 to 84, and higher scores indicate a stronger tendency to use defensive pessimism. If you score above 50, you would qualify as a defensive pessimist in my studies. If you score below 30, you would qualify as a strategic optimist.

If you score between 30 and 50, you may use _both_ strategies, or _neither_ strategy consistently. How you score will be influenced by the kind of situation you were thinking about when you answered the questions, because you may use different strategies in different situations.

We aren't just pessimists or optimists; we are pessimists who are anxious, conscientious, personable, good at math (or perhaps not), with long histories of relationships and experiences with siblings, parents, friends, lovers, and coworkers. We may be pessimists who are pessimistic only about relationships, or pessimistic about everything *but* relationships. People do not manifest just one or two simple, unrelated characteristics; instead, we have complex personality structures that develop and change with experience. Whether we're pessimistic about the job interview tomorrow depends on whether it's our first or fifth or hundredth, whether previous interviews have gone well or not, whether we've had similar jobs before or are trying to break into a new field, whether we really need the job or are just looking around, whether we're usually anxious meeting new people or comfortable in any situation, and even on whether we're talking about it to our best friend, our children, or the person with whom we're scheduling the interview.

All of this real-life complexity underlies the complexity in terminology that we've just reviewed. Looking (uncharacteristically for me) on the bright side, however, the overlap in terminology is not meaningless, because all of the phenomena described above are related, even if they are not identical. The complexity of our terminology reflects the complexity of real people, and it may remind us that to understand what people are doing and why, we need to avoid thinking of them just in terms of isolated characteristics—as one-dimensional optimists or pessimists.

LOOKING AT PESSIMISM and anxiety provides a perfect illustration of the need to consider the relationship among different aspects of personality. Defensive pessimism would make little sense if we didn't know that the people who use it are anxious and that anxiety creates particular problems for those who experience it. In the next chapter, I'll consider how defensive pessimists face the complexity that anxiety adds to their lives. We'll follow Katherine as she copes with her anxiety and hear Bill's partner, Daniel, describe his struggles, too. The experiences of Katherine and Daniel, and the research that corroborates them, illustrate how defensive pessimism functions as a powerful tool.

3

What It's All About

THE PROBLEM OF ANXIETY

The pious pretense that evil does not exist only makes it vague, enormous, and menacing.

—ALEISTER CROWLEY

Denial ain't just a river in Egypt.

—MARK TWAIN

WHY DOES ANXIETY INTERFERE?

The kind of anxiety that Katherine feels is not unusual; lots of people are anxious in similar situations. Indeed, lots of people are anxious lots of the time. Even people who don't think of themselves as "anxious types" have usually felt some anxiety at some point in their lives. (Remember adolescence?)

Anxiety is no fun, and it can get in the way of our efforts to reach our goals. It impairs our cognitive performance because it makes it hard to concentrate on a task—or indeed, on anything except ourselves and our subjective state. Anxiety can make us forget what we've learned, lose the thread of a conversation, or miss key pieces of information that we need to understand a situation.

Like its cousin, fear, anxiety can manifest itself in physical symptoms (increased heart rate, increased blood pressure, sweating, and shaking), which are often apparent to ourselves and to everyone watching us. Chronic anxiety over long periods of time can impair immune system functioning and otherwise damage our health and shrink our capacity for normal lives. Phobia is an extreme form of anxiety that leads us to avoid the situations that arouse it; panic attacks in the face of anxiety make some people flee regardless of the cost. Claustrophobics, for instance, who fear confined spaces, may even injure themselves in their desperate attempts to escape from tight spaces when panicked. And agoraphobics, who fear open spaces, may become prisoners in their homes, afraid even to venture out to pick up the newspaper at the foot of the driveway.

Yet anxiety, like other negative emotions, does serve a purpose. The increased physiological arousal involved in anxiety and fear may facilitate adaptive "flight or fight" responses in dangerous situations. Some level of arousal is adaptive because it helps us pay attention to cues in the environment—and according to one of the few psychological constructs to have the status of a "law" (the Yerkes-Dodson Law), there is an optimal level of arousal for most tasks. Too little arousal (think of someone sleeping), and performance on almost any task is abysmal. Too much arousal (think of how you feel after that fifth cup of coffee), and performance shows serious declines.

What constitutes too much or too little arousal varies from individual to individual and from task to task. Subjectively, however, we can almost always tell when we are too aroused, because rather than simply experiencing a physical state of arousal or positive feelings of anticipation and excitement, we experience thoughts and feelings that we call anxiety. The man who's champing at the bit to fly off on a dream vacation is excited, not anxious, even though his physiological arousal may be similar to his neighbor's, who, because he is anxious (not excited), wishes desperately for a Valium before his business flight. Usually, we want anxious feelings to go away (though not always—not when we're falling in love, for example); if we can't banish those feelings, we'd at least like to figure out some way to keep our anxiety from interfering with our performance.

HOW DOES ANXIETY INTERFERE?

How might anxiety interfere with performance? One way (think "fight or flight" again) is when it leads us to run away from whatever is making us anxious. Sometimes that's an appropriate response: Sprinting out of the path of a speeding truck, or a herd of stampeding animals, or a garrulous coworker may be exactly what we need to do. At other times, however, running away is not a very good option: If your predator is faster than you are, for example, you may be better off freezing in place and trying to remain undetected. But staying presents a different challenge: You have to be able to *tolerate* the feelings of anxiety, which are likely to continue until the predator leaves (or eats you). Tolerating those terrors is tough.

Few of us are faced with situations involving literal predators these days. Still, even when we're faced with a nonlethal threat like a predatory coworker or the prospect of failure, vanquishing the powerful urge to run away when we feel anxious is no easy mandate. Thus, the first problem posed by anxiety is the problem of making ourselves stay in the game; we have to be able to tolerate the tension well enough to remain in whatever situation (or in pursuit of whatever goal) makes us anxious. Woody Allen got it right, at least for anxious people, when he said "80 percent of success in life is just showing up."

Even if we can tolerate staying, anxiety can still mess up performance. Quavering voices are embarrassing to public speakers and distracting to the audience; the awkward trips and spilled drinks of the socially anxious are at once poignant and off-putting. Sometimes too much physiological arousal can be completely disqualifying: Nobody patronizes dentists who tremble while wielding their drills.

Anxiety produces more than physiological effects. It also disrupts mental performance, and it does so because it interferes with the ability to concentrate. Anxious math students fail not because their hands are shaking so badly that they can't write down their answers but because, when they're supposed to be focusing on the speed of the two trains hurtling down the track, all they can think about is how nervous they are, how much they hate taking math tests, how flunking math will ruin their lives, and how everyone else looks so calm. Likewise, anxious actors fail not because they can't make the required physical gestures but because they're so intent on how much is riding on this role and on how humiliating it would be to have to return to Peoria after blowing a shot at Broadway that they can't remember their lines. So, even if we've managed to show up, we still have to figure out a way to shift our attention from our anxious selves and feelings to the task at hand.

Yet another way anxiety can interfere is that it can lead to a kind of tunnel vision psychologists call "premature cognitive narrowing," which happens when we zoom in on a problem so narrowly that we constrain our repertoire of alternative solutions. Our poor, anxious math student has to guard against the tendency to use only one way of thinking about those pesky story problems, because the same techniques he used to solve problems involving trains heading to Chicago may not work when he has to determine the area of an irregularly shaped object. Premature cognitive narrowing can interfere with creativity, pacing, and understanding the possibilities in a given situation.

Anxiety has created an impressive set of obstacles for the student to conquer: To get through the test successfully he not only has to sit down and get himself to remember his algebra, but he also must look through a sufficiently wide-angled lens to recognize when he needs algebra, when he needs geometry, and when he needs to finish because everyone else has left and the janitor is about to lock the doors. And all this is *after* he made himself show up for the exam in the first place.

How Do Defensive Pessimists Manage Anxiety?

Katherine has always been a slightly nervous person. She's always been especially anxious about achievement types of situations—the kind where she has to demonstrate her ability, knowledge, or competence—but she's also always been ambitious and has high standards for herself. She wants to do the kind of professional work that she's doing, which means that she must sometimes face situations that make her anxious.

She has to be able to present her work at professional conferences and to submit papers for review by her peers so that she can obtain grant funding, publish her research, and get more grant funding. She must also perform as a teacher, where her competence is subject to her students' evaluations as well as her own.

Whenever she anticipates one of those situations, Katherine experiences familiar feelings in her stomach, and she's sure everything will end in a debacle. "The journal will never accept this paper. They'll hate my methodology." Or, referring to her invited address at a national convention, "What if I really blow it?"

That certainly is negative thinking, and it would be destructive thinking if it led Katherine to abandon her paper or not to show up for her invited address. This sort of thinking, however, is just the beginning of her strategy for managing her anxiety.

Because she knows that the top journal to which she wants to submit her research rejects almost 90 percent of all submissions, that her research methodology is controversial, and that peer review can be vicious, she prepares herself for rejection. This, then, is the pessimistic part of defensive pessimism: Katherine has high standards, and she sets low expectations.

It doesn't make her feel particularly cheerful to be pessimistic; after all, she would very much like for the paper to be accepted. But by lowering her expectations, Katherine has taken some of the pressure off herself, which in turn makes her feel somewhat less anxious. Anxiety is fundamentally an *anticipatory* emotion in that we're nervous about what's going to happen in the future. If we can reduce our feelings of uncertainty about the future by convincing ourselves that we know what will happen—even if our certainty is that things will end badly—we, like Katherine, can reduce anticipation and, thus, our anxiety.

Research shows (and our own experience may confirm) that *expected* disappointments, while still unpleasant, are easier to bear than unexpected disappointments. If we know what to expect, even if we expect the worst, we feel more in control. Being pessimistic allows Katherine to defuse the emotional power of the outcomes she is worried about, without ignoring or denying that they could happen. Her low expectations serve as a cognitive cushion that protects her, not to the extent that she won't feel bad if the paper isn't accepted, but enough that she can continue to work on it. Since that cushion allows her to go ahead and invest her effort rather than run away from the possibility of failure, her pessimism actually represents the first step in the management of her anxiety: "I know this is going to go badly. Now that I've got that settled, I can go ahead and get to work."

The Positive Power of Negative Thinking

NOT JUST PESSIMISM

Defensive pessimism is more than just pessimism. Setting low expectations—thinking that things may turn out badly—kicks off a reflective process of mentally playing through possible outcomes. This mental rehearsal—that obsessiveness of Katherine's to which I referred earlier—is the second component of the strategy. In other words, Katherine doesn't stop thinking after she declares that her paper will never get accepted. That pessimistic prediction just fuels her brainstorming about all the reasons why the paper might not get accepted and the details of how that could happen.

It's the "playing through" or mental rehearsal part of the strategy that leads Katherine's friends and colleagues to label her a worrywart—a name that implies that her worrying is both unnecessary and unproductive. They would be right if all Katherine did was to dither aimlessly and endlessly. But rather than being aimless, this process allows Katherine to dive into the nitty-gritty of what she has to do without being distracted by her anxiety. Mental rehearsal helps Katherine harness her anxiety and transform it into positive motivation.

While trying to work on her paper, she plays through a virtually comprehensive set of possible outcomes. She thinks about how a rival camp of researchers will probably be assigned to review the paper and will try to tear apart her statistical analyses, about how she may have entirely missed a body of literature that would be relevant, which will make her look ignorant, about how her main point is too complex. As she fleshes out these mental scenarios, she decides to have her graduate students double-check the statistics and to ask three of her colleagues to confirm that her literature review is complete and her argument crystal clear.

From the outside, her anguishing may seem like a big waste of energy and time. For someone who's anxious, however, and therefore vulnerable to the problems associated with premature cognitive narrowing, Katherine's kind of brainstorming about negative possibilities is protection against zooming in on only one or two details and squeezing out elements that count more. Minus her defensive pessimism, Katherine might easily bypass the large issue of the overall accessibility of her argument in favor of micro-analyzing her statistics—again.

By the time Katherine has exhausted the range of negative outcomes she can imagine, she's focusing more on the task at hand and less on her anxiety. She's succeeded in managing it so that she can concentrate and work effectively. Defensive pessimism has transformed the diffuse feelings of anxiety escalated by abstract and unelaborated "this-will-be-awful" scenarios into more concrete and less terrifying concerns about what might happen and what can be done to forestall it.

Katherine's mental rehearsal moves from general to specific possibilities, from abstract expectation of negative outcomes to disciplined consideration of *how* they could come about. From there, she proceeds to define plans for preventing negative outcomes and replacing them with positive ones. Her negative thinking is not passive rumination; it generates a clear and precise blueprint for action. That blueprint makes her feel more in control and, in turn, less vulnerable— at least in this situation—to further disruption by anxiety.

Not Just Planning

If it isn't obsessiveness or garden-variety worrying, is what Katherine does simply overly elaborate planning? Is the point of defensive pessimism simply that anxious people should plan well? Emphatically, no. That is not the point. Although they should plan well, that prescription for anxiety spectacularly misses the main point that defensive pessimism addresses, which is that anxiety interferes with planful thought. Anxious people can't plan well when they are anxious. They become distracted by irrelevancies and their own emotions, and they forget vital ingredients.

Defensive pessimists are able to use their pessimistic expectations and mental rehearsal to get to the stage where they can do effective planning—and once there, they can then go from plans to action. Without his defensive pessimism, our anxious host would fall victim to his anxiety and end up leaving the salt out of the quiche—even if he remembered to line up all the ingredients on the counter beforehand, in the middle of doing so he might rush off to check the tablecloth in the dryer or to call his date about bringing the wine, and his line-up would be incomplete. His dire imaginings of every potentially disastrous step of the party permit him to focus his thoughts and energies preemptively. As he envisions the distressed faces of guests biting into a tasteless pastry, his anxiety becomes specific and focused, and *consequently,* so does his planning.

One of the women I interviewed for this book told me a beautifully evocative story about how her anxieties about motherhood had left her unable to organize her thoughts. She had never thought of herself as an anxious person as a teenager or young adult, and her skills at coordinating and planning had been instrumental in getting her a job as an executive assistant at a major law firm—so she was shocked to find herself at such a loss at home. It took awhile, but she found a strategy that allowed her to regain a sense of control and to once again deploy the planning skills she'd had before: She became a defensive pessimist.

After her children were born, she discovered, "No way was I still in control. That illusion vanished forever." In its stead came an exponential growth in anxiety; suddenly, things that had never mattered before mattered. "An empty fridge, no clean clothes, running late—none of those things used to be a big deal. But now, they all have consequences for the

The Positive Power of Negative Thinking

kids. And that doesn't even count the big-time anxiety-makers, like when the kids get sick, or we have to arrange new childcare, or any of a million other things that come up all the time."

In response to this life transition, she ceased to assume that everything would turn out all right and began to prepare for the worst. Travel with her kids makes her especially anxious; one resultant fantasy has her stranded in a plane on the tarmac for hours, while her two young children are squirming and kicking the seats in front of them, howling with hunger and thirst, and pelting everyone around them with inedible peanuts.

As she mentally rehearses these frightening scenarios while preparing for a trip with the kids, she can also imagine what might prevent each disaster; she then methodically makes a list of what she needs to pack. The woman who in the old days spent six weeks in Europe with only a small duffle now carefully stashes enough food to hold the family overnight in an airport, extra clothes in case of spills or accidents, and half the contents of the toy box and bookshelf, fitting it all into backpacks that leave her hands and her husband's free to hold on to one kid apiece. She is anxious all the while she is packing, but once they are en route, she is able to concentrate on helping the kids to enjoy the trip, come what may.

Before she became a mother, she had felt in control from the beginning of whatever she was doing (traveling, throwing a party, coordinating her bosses' schedules) and had planned naturally and automatically, without giving a thought to how she did it. Now, she has to plan, but she also has to figure out *how* to plan, when anxiety keeps getting in the way. Feeling anxious and out of control has made planning hard, and only by rehearsing her nightmare scenarios has she been able to organize her thoughts well enough to plan and act effectively.

Defensive pessimism isn't different from good planning in terms of the ultimate results. It is different because of its role in getting to those results: Defensive pessimism is the process that *allows* anxious people to do good planning. They can't plan effectively until they control their anxiety. They have to go through their worst-case scenarios and exhaustive mental rehearsal in order to start the process of planning, carry it through effectively, and then get from planning to *doing*.

4

Why Can't a Pessimist
Be More Like an Optimist?

Don't ever become a pessimist . . . a pessimist is correct oftener than an optimist, but an optimist has more fun.

—ROBERT A. HEINLEIN

For every complex problem, there is a solution that is simple, neat, and wrong.

—HENRY L. MENCKEN

*I*f you recognized yourself in the descriptions of Katherine or the traveling mother, you're probably already convinced that defensive pessimism is a coherent strategy that works, and you don't need more "proof." If you're more like Bill, though, you may be skeptical. Those who are more positive and less anxious often have trouble believing that defensive pessimism can really have positive results. For them, data from an empirical research program provides a wedge that opens the way to understanding what it is like to be a defensive pessimist.

In the spirit of elucidation, then, this chapter offers support for my descriptions of defensive pessimism by summarizing research that addresses many of the questions I hear from those who have doubts about how defensive pessimism works. Those questions usually focus on whether defensive pessimists really "need" to be so negative—in their expectations, in their mental rehearsal, and in their general mood. As Bill once put it, "Why can't a defensive pessimist be more like an optimist?"

It's been a challenge to design research that really gets at these questions. To get evidence that reveals the inner workings of defensive pessimism, we need to be able to expose the *process* by which people harness their anxiety to achieve a given outcome. We can measure *what* people have done, after they have done it, but how do we get at *how* they did it?

Our research team decided to systematically interfere with each of the components of defensive pessimism we'd identified, because one way to show how something normally works to produce a specific outcome is to interfere with that something and show that the outcome changes accordingly. If we raise defensive pessimists' expectations, making them more optimistic, what happens? If we distract them from their mental rehearsal or relax them so they're less anxious, what happens? The upshot of all this research is straightforward: Defensive pessimism helps anxious people perform better, and attempts to interfere with any part of their strategy messes up their performance.

CAN'T DEFENSIVE PESSIMISTS JUST "LOOK ON THE BRIGHT SIDE"?

We know that seeing the glass half empty is only one component of defensive pessimism. Maybe defensive pessimists don't really need to be pessimistic. Could they perform just as well (or even better) if we could get them to be more optimistic? It is possible that their pessimism is "epiphenomenal," something that goes along for the ride, and doesn't really have anything to do with their anxiety or their performance.

This question became the focus of one of our early experiments on defensive pessimism, which demonstrated that the defensive pessimists' pessimism really did work in positive ways. We identified and invited defensive pessimists and strategic optimists into a psychology laboratory to work on tasks that were similar to standardized aptitude tests. These participants were successful students at a competitive university, so they all "realistically" could have expected to perform very well.

Why Can't a Pessimist Be More Like an Optimist?

Before they began, we measured how much anxiety and control they felt over the upcoming tasks. At that point, the defensive pessimists felt significantly more anxious and less in control than the strategic optimists, just as we had predicted. We asked half of the participants how well they thought they would do on the tasks. The defensive pessimists set low expectations for their performance—significantly lower than those of the strategic optimists—even though both groups had comparable abilities. In other words, the defensive pessimists were pessimistic, again, as predicted.

We told the other half of the participants that we had looked over their records and knew that they would do well, "preempting" their own expectations, in the hope that the authority of our observation would manipulate them into setting more positive expectations than they otherwise would have. The defensive pessimists in this half of the group actually did set higher expectations than those in the other half who were allowed to predict without interference from the experimenter.

Up to this point, the study shows only that defensive pessimists tend to be pessimistic and that they are not immune to the manipulations of tricky researchers. The participants' actual performance came next, and that's the key part of the study. We found that when defensive pessimists were optimistic, their performance suffered, whereas they did just fine if left to their pessimism. Remember that the defensive pessimists started out being anxious and that the kind of tasks they performed were the same kind of tasks that anxiety disrupts. The anxious defensive pessimists who used their typical pessimistic strategy performed well, and their anxiety didn't interfere with their performance. But when we took away their pessimism, we didn't take away their anxiety. Instead, we disabled a key component of their strategy.

CAN'T DEFENSIVE PESSIMISTS JUST GET THEIR MINDS OFF THEIR WORRIES?

Maybe defensive pessimists "need" their pessimism, but do they really need all that mental rehearsal, too? Could they just be pessimistic and then "chill out," dispensing with their worst-case scenarios and obsessive preparation?

To explore the role of mental rehearsal, we told defensive pessimists that they were going to complete intelligence test–type tasks (as before). Before their performance, we asked half of the group to list all the possible outcomes they could think of for their upcoming performance. We distracted the other half with a clerical project that required their attention and prevented them from engaging in their usual reflective process.

We questioned both groups about how anxious they were and how in control they felt as they anticipated the tasks

Why Can't a Pessimist Be More Like an Optimist?

ahead. We also hooked them up to equipment that monitored aspects of their physiological arousal, which is a common objective method of measuring anxiety as well as a way to monitor continuous changes throughout the experiment.

As expected, defensive pessimists reported being more anxious than strategic optimists, and they said they felt less in control. But despite their anxiety, they did at least as well as the optimists when we let them use their typical strategy. Their performance fell, however, when we interfered with their strategy by preventing them from reflecting about possible outcomes. Physiological arousal among the defensive pessimists who were using their strategy started high, peaked during their mental rehearsal, and then *decreased* before they actually had to perform. It is not surprising that anxiety did not interfere with their performance, because by the time they had to perform, they were no longer feeling very anxious. The reverse was true for the defensive pessimists who were prevented from mentally playing through outcomes; their anxiety was high initially, lower during the distraction task, and very high during their performance.

CAN'T DEFENSIVE PESSIMISTS "JUST RELAX" OR "THINK POSITIVELY"?

Once our studies confirmed that both pessimism and mental rehearsal play important roles in harnessing anxiety for defensive pessimists, we wondered whether harnessing that anxiety is beside the point. Given that their problem is anxiety, maybe defensive pessimists would be better off actively trying positive thinking or relaxation techniques to cope with their anxiety. The research showed otherwise.

Defensive pessimists' mental rehearsal resembles a coping imagery technique that sports psychologists use to prepare athletes for upcoming performances. For instance, a gymnast is asked to imagine every step in her routine and is coaxed to conjure up every possible detail about how a mistake might happen *and* how she would recover from it. The reasoning behind this technique is that it will help athletes to cope with anxiety and with whatever problems arise during a performance.

These same performance experts also use other, more positive imagery techniques, particularly "mastery coping," in which one imagines, in vivid detail, a *perfect* performance. Mastery imagery may help because when the mind rehearses perfect movements, the corresponding neuromuscular pathways are strengthened, which can make the correct actions more automatic and improve subsequent performance. Mastery imagery may also improve confidence by helping people believe that they are capable of performing well.

Relaxation techniques are also used to bolster performance. Those techniques usually involve consciously focusing

Why Can't a Pessimist Be More Like an Optimist?

on relaxing a series of muscles, listening to soothing music, or vividly imagining oneself in relaxing surroundings, such as sinking into the warm sand on a sunny tropical beach.

To explore whether mastery imagery or relaxation techniques might provide happier ways for defensive pessimists to manage their anxiety, we designed a study where participants tried to get their best score at playing darts after engaging in different kinds of mental imagery. Defensive pessimists in the study were randomly assigned to listen to one of three tapes before their dart game: a guided coping imagery tape (which is like the mental rehearsal that defensive pessimists typically do), a mastery imagery tape (which is positive thinking), or a relaxation imagery tape (which doesn't involve thinking about performance at all).

We measured anxiety and feelings of control before the imagery manipulations, and we found, as usual, that defensive pessimists were more anxious and felt less in control than strategic optimists. We were really most interested in their actual performance, though, and we found that defensive pessimists did not respond well to either mastery or relaxation imagery. They performed best when they listened to the coping imagery tape that mimicked what they usually do.

The participants in that study were mostly novices at dart throwing, but we found the same pattern of results when we repeated the study with members of a collegiate rowing team—all experienced, excellent athletes—who happened to be defensive pessimists. Indeed, as expertise increases, the influence of emotion and mental control on performance becomes more critical. Among Olympic athletes, the ability to handle the pressure in elite competition can be the crucial determinant of the .001 second or .01 point that distinguishes the gold medal winner from the runner-up.

This is not to say that only defensive pessimists are able to control their anxiety or that there are no other effective strategies people can adopt. However, this research supports the view that there are individual differences in how people best manage their anxiety, even among—or perhaps *especially* among—the cream of the crop.

FROM THE LABORATORY TO REAL LIFE

Throwing darts and working on aptitude tests are not relevant to the lives of most people, so we designed a study to determine whether people use defensive pessimism in the real world the same way they do in a psychology laboratory. We also studied adults of various ages, in case our results from studies of college students (a convenient sample for college professors) were unique to that age group.

Relying on a research technique called "experience sampling," we captured slices from real-life psychological processes. Our participants agreed to carry electronic pagers that were

Why Can't a Pessimist Be More Like an Optimist?

programmed to beep on a random schedule, about five times a day. They filled out a brief report every time they heard the beep, writing down what they were doing, who they were with, how they were feeling, and whether their activity of the moment was relevant to any of their personal goals.

Defensive pessimists and strategic optimists were given one of two different forms to fill out when they heard the beep. The forms were identical, except that one section on half of the forms included a question asking the participants to reflect on how much progress they were making toward their goals at that particular time, which we thought would launch the defensive pessimists' typical mental rehearsal but would interfere with the strategic optimists' attempts to distract themselves.

All of the participants—female graduate nursing students ranging in age from twenty-three to sixty-three—were leading busy, complicated lives. Their goals ranged from "saving to buy a house" to "rescuing a nephew from life on the streets" to "being promoted to supervisor at the hospital" to "exploring new interests after a divorce." As they reported on their daily lives, their specific situations reflected the diversity of their life contexts and resources (money, social support, time).

Stopping to reflect on their goals in the middle of whatever they were doing appeared to help the defensive pessimists (and only the defensive pessimists), focusing them so that they were able to direct their efforts productively. Indeed, the defensive pessimists who were prompted to be more reflective during their daily lives reported feeling less anxious, were more satisfied with their efforts, and made more progress toward their goals than those who were not prompted. The results of this study reassure us that the impact of strategies on performance in the lab is analogous to the impact of strategies on real-life goals.

CAN'T DEFENSIVE PESSIMISTS JUST BE HAPPY?

Being optimistic, distracting oneself, thinking positively, and trying to relax don't seem to help defensive pessimists perform well. Maybe that's because all of those things are too cerebral: They focus too much on thinking. Maybe the way to help defensive pessimists with their anxiety problem is to cheer them up: If they're happy, surely they won't be anxious. To anyone but a defensive pessimist, that might seem like a good idea, but our research showed that for defensive pessimists, being happy also interferes with performance. (This certainly doesn't mean they are never happy or are usually unhappy—but we'll get to that later.)

How we think and how we feel are intimately connected, so it makes sense to look at how defensive pessimists' moods influence their strategy and performance. For our first study, we didn't try to change people's moods, but we measured the mood they were in when they arrived for the study. Defensive pessimists were in significantly more negative moods than strategic optimists as they began the study. We then had them try to solve different kinds of puzzles involving words and numbers. For defensive pessimists, negative mood related to *better* performance, and positive mood related to *worse* performance.

When we actually manipulated mood, using music to induce positive or negative moods, we learned that it was *possible* to make the defensive pessimists feel more positive, but when they felt better, the defensive pessimists performed more *poorly* than when they were in a negative mood. In other words, we could cheer them up, but only at the expense of their subsequent performance.

DON'T MESS WITH MY STRATEGY— I'M DOING FINE ON MY OWN

These studies highlight how low expectations and mental rehearsal help defensive pessimists harness their anxiety so that it does not impair their performance. Other researchers have gotten very similar results using different kinds of mood simulations and different ways of influencing how people think. This research converges to reinforce what defensive pessimists say, which is that "just relaxing," "looking on the bright side," and "cheering up" are not the answers for them, even though they often have to contend with other people who try to "help" them.

Bill's partner, Daniel, is anxious about both achievement and social situations. He knows that people (including Bill) often wish that he were more optimistic, but he also knows that, for him, optimism is artificial and risky. Daniel describes how his family always tries to psych him up before an important event:

> They offer loads of encouragement, because they want to make me feel better. The first couple of times this happened when I was in college, I really responded. I went into my test feeling very up and hardly worried at all. It was like having my own cheerleading squad. But then when I had to actually answer the questions, my mind went blank and I felt panicky, and of course they weren't there to help. Now I realize that I have to trust my own feelings. Sometimes I pretend to feel confident to make them feel better, but behind the mask I still worry. I don't want them to "fix" my attitude; I just want to be able to deal with my worries and psych myself up my own way.

Katherine is also on to something when she insists that her way of going about things works for her and that she is not "needlessly" worrying but rather worrying for a reason. She needs to be able to regulate her anxiety in order to prevent

Why Can't a Pessimist Be More Like an Optimist?

immobilization or disruption of performance. She does not need to be "cured" of her defensive pessimism; instead, her defensive pessimism is her solution to the problem of anxiety.

Strategies as Alternative Tools

Anxious people who use defensive pessimism seem to be doing a kind of cognitive therapy on themselves—and doing it well. Their strategy is in sync with techniques of diverse professional therapists and counselors. But defensive pessimism is not the only strategy that individuals develop for dealing with anxiety. Indeed, there are a number of creative techniques or strategies. As we begin to consider those strategies and how they compare, it is worth taking a moment to unpack what it means to call something a strategy—or perhaps more importantly, what it *does not* mean.

A strategy is a coherent pattern of expectations, appraisals, planning, effort, and retrospection that unfolds over time while in pursuit of personally relevant goals. It describes a person's typical or characteristic way of dealing with a specific kind of problem or of working toward a particular goal. Looking at strategies as part of people's personalities doesn't mean looking just at what they do one time in one situation or looking at their isolated expectations, moods, explanations, or behaviors. Madly rushing to the grocery store one Friday evening after work because your kids called with a last-minute chance to go camping over the weekend and you need to get them supplies doesn't reveal much about your strategies for raising your kids or for planning your weekends.

Even if you are typically rushing, that isn't really a strategy—it's just a typical behavior. Without knowing more about what you're feeling or thinking or trying to do—what all that rushing is directed toward or in the service of and whether that's how you usually approach that kind of thing—we can't know whether it is part of a strategy or just a by-product of temporary overscheduling or an active temperament. Even tearing around four Fridays in a row to prepare for weekend plans that you've known about several days in advance doesn't necessarily reveal a strategy; it probably just means that you haven't yet developed a coherent strategy for this kind of situation—which is often the case during life transitions like motherhood, as our traveling mother discovered.

On the other hand, if every Friday is a frantic dash to prepare for weekend plans, we begin to get the sense that there's a strategy at work. If we then find out that you hate the thought of sitting idle and that keeping on the move helps you feel like you're accomplishing things, then we begin to get a sense that there's a strategy at work and that rushing from task to task is one element in that strategy, which is defined or outlined when we know your goals.

Why Can't a Pessimist Be More Like an Optimist?

———

This use of the term strategy is similar to, but not identical to, uses of the term outside of psychology. Typically, when we speak of strategies—techniques we develop to approach an intimidating boss, to counter an opponent in chess, or to develop a marketing angle for a new product—we are referring to *conscious* strategies. We assume that people are aware of choosing to approach a problem in a particular way.

When we talk about playing chess, that assumption probably holds. Whether we refer to the strategies of the masters, celebrated in books and taught to generations of students, or the strategies of novices, which might reduce to "try to remember where all my pieces are," we're describing deliberate thoughts and choices. We also assume that, once they're described clearly, almost anyone can learn various strategies for chess—at least with enough hard work.

However, when we talk about strategies for living that are part of personality, like defensive pessimism and strategic optimism, the presumption that our strategies are conscious or deliberate doesn't always hold. People may be aware of the strategies they use, and they may even consciously work to develop their strategies, but that is by no means always the case, as we will see in the next chapter when we meet Jeff and Mindy, whose strategies are less than successful. They will also remind us that strategies are not synonymous with good solutions. People are quite capable both of using bad strategies—

The Positive Power of Negative Thinking

in life as in chess—and of using strategies badly, by employing them in inappropriate situations.

THE TOOLBOX METAPHOR is an apt one; theoretically at least, people may have many strategies in a repertoire, just as there are many tools in a toolbox. Katherine, for example, is much more optimistic about her relationships than about her work, and she is so optimistic when it comes to her finances that she borders on whimsy. She isn't a defensive pessimist all the time, to the exclusion of anything else. Referring to her as a defensive pessimist is in part a rhetorical convenience. Yet it also reflects the reality that defensive pessimism as a response to anxiety is such a salient part of her life that it has become a defining element of her personality. It is not the only tool in her toolbox, but it may be the one she uses most frequently in public, and thus it is the one that most people see first as they get to know her.

In that sense, people may "become" their strategies. Indeed, if you usually use only one strategy, your proficiency with alternatives either never develops or atrophies over time. An apprentice carpenter whose sole assignment is to pound nails may never have learned how to handle a saw well; even if he once knew how, he's likely to make a mess the first few times he uses it again after being out of practice for so long. Especially since Katherine's defensive pessimism works so well for her, she has had little incentive to look for alternative strategies at work. She would be hard-pressed at this point in her career to imagine other ways of doing what she does; even if offered suggestions, she would hesitate to give up the strategy she knows and is expert at for something unknown that she would have to learn from scratch.

Even if most people use only a couple of strategies regularly, rather than having a large repertoire in constant readiness, the toolbox metaphor is useful because it reminds us that strategies have to be understood in the context of the goals and intentions of those who use them. To understand—and evaluate—whether our carpenter is using the right tool when he picks up a saw, we need to know whether he's still trying to pound nails or whether he now needs to cut a forty-five-degree angle in a piece of wood. Once we've determined what he's trying to do, we can see whether he's chosen the best tool for the job; a saw is surely a better choice than a hammer for cutting the forty-five-degree angle, but whether it's the best choice will depend on whether there's a miter box available. We've already seen that for those who need to manage their anxiety, strategic optimism is not a helpful tool; whether defensive pessimism is the right tool for particular people will depend on whether they feel anxious *and* on what kind of alternative strategies they may know.

The Positive Power of Negative Thinking

The toolbox metaphor also highlights the importance of considering how well people are able to select from among available strategies in a given situation—that is, to select the right tool for the task. Even if our beleaguered carpenter has a hammer, a saw, and a miter box in his toolbox, he has to know what each does best, both in theory and when the wood is in his hands. Katherine, our expert defensive pessimist, is likely to find that her strategy fails her if she can't recognize when she should turn it off and adopt another approach; if every classroom lecture, every meeting with a student—even every trip to the grocery store—precipitates extensive mental rehearsal, she'll exhaust herself and every one around her, and the payoff (especially from the grocery store trip) won't be enough to compensate for the effort. (Similarly, she might benefit from realizing that her optimism about money is somewhat misguided and that her defensive pessimism could be a good way to control the distance between her income and her expenditures.)

Arguing that defensive pessimism is a good tool for the task of managing anxiety does not mean that it is a perfect solution. As with most strategies, there are costs to using defensive pessimism, as well as benefits. The next chapter will focus on the benefits, which are highlighted when we compare anxious people who use defensive pessimism with anxious people who use other strategies: Enter the avoider and the self-handicapper.

5

Taking Cover

THE AVOIDER AND
THE SELF-HANDICAPPER

Our doubts are traitors, and make us lose the good
we oft might win by fearing to attempt.

—WILLIAM SHAKESPEARE

Running away will never make you free.

—KENNY LOGGINS

*J*eff has some things in common with Katherine and Daniel.
Like them, he is very bright and very anxious. Because of his
anxiety, Jeff faces the same problem they do: He needs to find
a way to manage that anxiety. But Jeff has developed a strategy
that contrasts vividly with defensive pessimism. Unlike Daniel
and Katherine, he doesn't have to worry about big presenta-

tions or proposals at work, because whenever he is threatened by the prospect of advancement to a job where such things are required, he quits and looks for another entry-level job. Jeff's strategy is, whenever possible, in whatever ways are necessary, to avoid being in situations that make him anxious.

Jeff's inclination to avoid anxiety-arousing situations is not unusual. One of the most common reactions to anxiety is avoidance; we run away from whatever makes us feel anxious. As I've already noted, there are plenty of times (for example, dark alleys with lurking strangers, toxic relationships) where steering clear in the first place or withdrawing as quickly as possible is appropriate and effective. But avoidance can take other forms besides literally running away—some of which are subtle and difficult to identify. And avoidance can also create its own kind of self-perpetuating traps.

Two familiar avoidant strategies—one of them more blatant than the other, and both of them tools for coping with anxiety—are literal avoidance and self-handicapping. When people use either of these strategies, they are running away. Often they are running away from a specific and potent source of anxiety: *the threat to self-esteem presented by the possibility of failure.*

THE AVOIDER

Since college, Jeff has worked in a corporate mailroom and has been assistant manager of a drugstore; now thirty-two, he is temping for a New York agency. Jeff started out with high SAT scores and thought he might want to become a doctor, but early in his academic career, he began to oversleep, miss class, and slack off. He took an introductory course or two from almost every department and major-hopped as soon as the courses got tougher. His credits were so scattered that he graduated only when a creative advisor retroactively designed an individualized major called "Natural and Cultural Studies" around them.

Jeff can't decide what he wants to do in either his professional or his personal life, and he is less successful than Katherine, Daniel, or Bill. He has trouble explaining to his mystified family and friends why he finds it so hard to commit to anything, but the bottom line is that he is anxious, especially in what we might think of as achievement situations. He knows he has done pretty well in school, but he has never known quite why or been confident that he can replicate past successes at will. Parents and teachers often praised his intelligence, but Jeff could never understand why they were so convinced of his ability, when every time he sat down to write a paper he had no idea how it would turn out. In college, his increasing anxiety about his ability to succeed led to insomnia, headaches, loneliness, social withdrawal, and eventually to an overwhelming desire to escape from the pressure.

Taking Cover

Jeff has sacrificed virtually all his other goals to the over-arching one of avoiding that pressure, that terrifying feeling of anxiety that arises whenever he is faced with a challenge or a risk. As his friends have begun to advance in their fields and build their families, he has tried to convince himself that his lifestyle is free from the stress and responsibility that sometimes seem to overwhelm their lives. But he doesn't really feel free at all; he feels trapped and stressed in his daily life by the constant struggle to pay his bills and by a general sense that he is being left behind. Paradoxically, in trying to avoid anxiety, he has created a life that is at once profoundly unsatisfying and *anxiety-provoking*.

JEFF'S APPROACH TO his own anxiety gives us a feel for the costs involved in using avoidance as a strategy. He tries to confine his life to contexts in which he feels no pressure, but avoiding anxiety-producing situations requires that he remain constantly on the lookout for precisely those things that make him anxious. That constant vigilance is exhausting, and it takes energy away from other endeavors.

Jeff has to watch himself so he doesn't get too involved with his coworkers. He doesn't dare to like them too much, because he knows his temporary position will end soon, and attachment to people there would only make leaving harder. He also has to make sure they don't get to know him too well. If they like him and believe that he is smart and capable, they might try to get him to stay in a permanent position, which would involve much more responsibility and risk of failure, and he doesn't want to face that. Just the anticipation of a casual "Wanna come to the coffeehouse with us after work?" from someone in the next cubicle is threatening enough that Jeff will cut out early on Friday afternoon just to avoid it.

Jeff has set up his life so that he spends all his efforts to achieve an absence of (short-term) *negative* outcomes, but that means he doesn't have many *positive* outcomes (short-term or long-term). By staying in temporary jobs, Jeff ensures that he won't have to put himself on the line in any big assignments that he might have trouble completing well (his lack of confidence doesn't extend to typing, filing, and running errands)—so he successfully avoids tremendous, acute anxiety and the potential for big humiliations. But he also avoids making new friends and having fun on the job, lacks the financial and psychological advantages of job security, and gives up the opportunity to learn new skills, grow more confident, and experience intense satisfaction.

As long he sticks to avoidance as his primary strategy, Jeff's future is unlikely to be brighter than his present. The longer he avoids anything that might challenge his self-image, the more difficult it is to sustain the self-deception

Taking Cover

necessary to maintain his fragile self-concept. When he was newly graduated and only twenty-two, it was easy for him to believe that he had untapped potential and might someday be great. At thirty-two, he finds it harder to find consolation in the idea of his future potential, but he can still convince himself that there are major advantages to being young and unencumbered. At forty-five, he is likely to find it extremely difficult to prop up a belief in his own potential as he types correspondence for thirty-five-year-old executives and drifts through a new office every week, without colleagues, outside endeavors, or close friends to sustain him.

Yet if he stops avoiding and adopts a more realistic self-view, without other coping strategies to handle his anxiety, he's also at risk for becoming helpless or hopeless. His first attempts—like most first attempts—to confront his anxiety are likely to fall short, and initial failure may convince him that his doubts were well founded and that he is a failure.

Much of what we learn, from specific skills like handling a difficult technical problem to more general life skills like handling criticism from others, we learn through direct experience. We learn by trying, and sometimes, by failing. If, like Jeff, we avoid those situations that make us anxious, we are also avoiding opportunities to fail and to learn how to handle failure. We don't get better at dealing with those situations, and we don't get less anxious about them. Experience—knowing

The Positive Power of Negative Thinking

what to expect from both situations and ourselves—is one of the most effective treatments for anxiety, but it is precisely the kind of treatment precluded by Jeff's attempts to avoid anything new and challenging.

Jeff's particular brand of avoidance isn't the only way that people end up exacerbating their anxiety and increasing the probability of negative outcomes by using strategies that temporarily dampen uncomfortable emotions. Extremely shy people will sometimes go to great lengths to avoid social interactions (especially those involving strangers and members of the opposite sex). Of course, by avoiding anxiety this way, they cheat themselves of the opportunity to meet people who might become friends and intimates, even though they really want those relationships. They also cheat themselves of the opportunity to develop the social skills that ease interactions. Meanwhile, those interactions they cannot avoid continue to be negative, which confirms their perceptions that they are undesirable and fuels a cycle that fosters anxiety about future social interactions.

Where avoidance eases anxiety—as it does for Jeff, whose strategy for managing his fear of failure prevents him from trying, learning, and succeeding—it does so at considerable, paradoxical cost. For the socially anxious, that cost is the creation of a negative cycle of continued social isolation.

Taking Cover

THE SELF-HANDICAPPER

People do develop other strategies less extreme than complete avoidance to reduce their anxiety so that they can at least be involved in those situations that make them anxious, yet avoid confirmation of their worst fears about themselves. One of the most common strategies for dealing with anxiety is called *self-handicapping*. Many of us will squirm a bit as we recognize aspects of self-handicapping in our own behavior, because it is a common strategy across a wide variety of situations. Probably few of us reach adulthood without relying on some self-handicaps along the way.

Some anxious individuals, however, don't just resort to self-handicapping on scattered occasions; they self-handicap almost all the time in situations that are central to their lives. Just as Katherine and Daniel represent defensive pessimist "types" because of the pivotal role defensive pessimism plays in their lives, those who regularly rely on self-handicapping to handle anxiety become a type, like Mindy.

Mindy works in advertising. Like Bill and Katherine, Mindy is highly educated and has a good job, but unlike them, she is always stressed and behind schedule. She is eager to take on new projects, but as deadlines approach, she usually has to stay up all night, frantically trying to get everything ready. Her friends have become accustomed to her apologetic cancellations because she is too behind schedule. Mindy is not just behind relative to specific deadlines at work; she also feels chronically behind because she never quite manages to get to the other projects and goals in her life, like having more time for her friends or finding time to exercise.

If you were to watch Mindy from a distance, it would be hard to figure out why she is always so behind, because she seems always to be working. She spends even more time on e-mail than Bill; but somehow she doesn't manage to respond in time to her most important messages. Every night she carries home a briefcase loaded with work, and her planner is crammed with appointments, "to do" lists, and Post-it notes to herself, but she is still always searching for better ways to organize in hopes of finally getting it all together.

Closer examination of this whirlwind of motion would reveal that Mindy is least likely to be working, at any given moment, on whatever project is closest to being due. She ruefully admits to procrastination and disorganization. She has a shelf full of books with advice about how to stop procrastinating and how to become more organized, but somehow the tickler files and color-coded notes never seem to help her much—except that reading about them and going to the office supply store are two of her favorite ways to procrastinate.

Mindy does not fully recognize that her disorganization and procrastination are really *strategies* for managing her anxiety about her performance at work. (In fact, self-handicapping only works if we are not clearly aware that we're doing it.) If you were to ask her whether work makes her anxious, she might say yes; but if you asked her why, she would say that she just has too much work, not that she is concerned about whether she can do her work well.

But Mindy has doubts about whether she is really intelligent, creative, and capable enough to do consistently good work, and those doubts make her feel anxious. When she thinks about working on the next project that is due, her anxiety increases. That's when she distracts herself by writing e-mails to old friends, filing ancient memos, or rearranging her Rolodex—anything that will get her mind off the task at hand and the potential for failure that it represents. Typically, at the last minute, the need to hand something in will overcome her anxiety about the quality of her work; she will rally and put forth an heroic effort, which is often enough to prevent disaster.

Mindy's strategy for managing her anxiety is one example of self-handicapping. Self-handicapping is when people preemptively provide themselves (and others) with an explanation for their performance that will make it less incriminating if the performance does not go well. For Mindy, procrastination and disorganization provide a handicap or an "out": If her proposals do not pass muster at work, it is not because she lacks creativity or ability, it is just because she threw them to-gether at the last minute. She would much rather have people think of her—and she would much rather think of herself—as scatterbrained or overcommitted than as more fundamentally incompetent. In her mind (and, she hopes, in the minds of those who work with her), the fact that her proposals are often successful, *even though* she rushed to get them ready, serves to prove how bright she really is. After all, just imagine how brilliant her work *could* be if she just got organized and gave it the attention, time, and effort she should.

Self-handicapping sounds a lot like making excuses. It involves a particular kind of excuse, though, because it is pre-emptive: Self-handicaps provide *potential* excuses, before we even know whether we will need them.

Protective Attributions

As thinking beings, we naturally want to make the world more comprehensible and predictable, so we try to figure out not only what happens but *why* things happen. For example, we say to ourselves, "They broke up because they were always arguing," or "I lost that contract because no one could do what they wanted for that amount of money." How a particular event reflects on us—what it means about our abilities, what it implies about our futures—depends in part on the explanations we make about that event. The causal attributions we develop for our experiences are important because they influence how we feel about those experiences and ourselves, and they influence our motivation in future situations.

People in Western cultures typically make four general types of attributions: attributions to ability, effort, task difficulty, and luck. We may think, for example, that the reason we got a promotion was because of our obviously superior sales ability, our incredibly hard work, or some combination of the two. Or, we may think that the promotion happened because Uncle Harry is a member of the board of directors. In the former case, we are attributing our achievements to personal, internal factors. In the latter case, we are attributing our promotion to external causes.

Attributions can also differ in the extent to which they refer to causes that remain stable over time or to causes that we believe change over time. In Western culture, we tend to believe that abilities—intelligence, athletic prowess, musical talent—are relatively stable characteristics inherent in individuals. If we think a child is smart, we assume she will grow into a smart adult. In contrast, we perceive effort as much less stable; formerly hard-working people may slack off at some point in the future or vice versa.

Attributional theorists also characterize attributions according to how *specific* or *general* they are, which influences how pervasive the implications of those attributions are.

When we repair a flat tire in record time, our explanation may focus on the specific ("I was so fast because I am good at fixing flat tires") or the general ("I was so fast because I am good at all mechanical things").

Self-handicapping allows us to make attributions that are less negative if things go badly, because attributions to more external, unstable, or specific causes will be less personally threatening than attributions to more internal, stable, and general causes. If Mindy can blame a badly written presentation on the fact that she had to write it in the taxi on the way to the meeting, that attribution is less internal, less stable, and less general—and less painful—than the attribution that she is a bad writer.

In both cases she might feel rotten because the presentation didn't go well, but if she can "explain away" that bad outcome, she won't feel *as* bad; in particular, she won't feel as bad *about herself*. Plus, the next time she faces the task of writing a presentation, she won't be demoralized by the belief that she is a bad writer, which if true, would imply that future presentations would go just as badly as the previous one had. Her attributions for negative events are, in this way, *self-protective;* they shield her from the potential fallout from failure.

Self-handicapping can also be *self-enhancing;* that is, not only can it protect our self-esteem, but it can even increase our positive self-perceptions. In the case of the badly written presentation, Mindy's self-handicapping before the fact allows her to make protective attributions; but if the presentation goes well, she is in a position to make quite flattering attributions to more stable, internal, and general causes: "If I can pull off a successful presentation in those circumstances, I must really be a brilliant writer!"

In attributional terms, then, self-handicappers set themselves up to feel okay regardless of how things turn out. If things go badly, they can make self-protective attributions. If things go well, they can make self-enhancing attributions. In this sense, there are benefits to self-handicapping as a strategy.

When Mindy self-handicaps at work, she would like to avoid failure, but it is even more critical that she avoid seeing herself as intrinsically incapable of success. For Mindy to stay in the situation at all, she faces the same problem as Katherine, Daniel, and Jeff: She needs to be able to control her anxiety about feedback that would confirm a negative self-image. Her handicaps provide her with a particular kind of cognitive cushion; knowing beforehand that she has an excuse ready if things go badly allows her to go forward.

Alternative Handicaps

Procrastination and disorganization are not the only ways to self-handicap. Some psychologists argue that drug and alcohol use qualify. One experiment showed that students who were anxious were more likely to choose to take a drug they believed would impair their performance before a test than students who were not anxious; if they did poorly, they could point to the drug as the cause.

Other seemingly odd choices may also be the result of self-handicapping. Studies have shown that students high in the tendency to self-handicap were more likely to listen to music that they were told would *interfere* with their performance than to music they were told would enhance their performance, especially if they believed performance was a good measure of their innate ability.

"Symptom-claiming" is also a form of self-handicapping. If we can convince ourselves and whatever audience might be relevant that we experience symptoms that interfere with doing our best, then the symptoms—rather than our ability—become the focus of explanations for our performance. We might even claim anxiety itself as a symptom: "Even though I know I can play the part, I blew the audition because I got so nervous I choked up and couldn't show my stuff."

Researchers who study self-handicapping distinguish between claimed self-handicaps and behavioral self-handicaps. The former includes things we tell others and ourselves (for example, we're too nervous or too tired to do well), whereas the latter refers to specific behaviors that are likely to make outcomes worse (for example, taking drugs or not practicing). Thinking about the different kinds of handicaps people may adopt helps us to see the potential costs and benefits of self-handicapping. Generally, claimed self-handicaps are relatively low risk compared to behavioral self-handicaps. If we tell everyone we have a stomachache before a presentation at work, our claim doesn't necessarily have any effect on our actual performance, and it still provides an excuse if we don't do well. If we come to the presentation having had a few drinks, however, that handicap, while obviously providing an explanation for a poor performance, also makes a poor performance much more likely.

Moreover, if people think our poor performance was caused by a stomachache, they are likely to be relatively forgiving: It could happen to anyone. On the other hand, we're likely to be held responsible for drinking or taking drugs. Being tipsy may confuse the attributions people make about our ability to deliver a presentation, but it is also very likely to lead to incriminating and negative attributions about our self-control, judgment, and professionalism.

RELATIVE TO OTHER kinds of self-handicaps, how effective are Mindy's generalized disorganization and procrastination? They are certainly more risky than claiming a stomachache on one occasion, in part because disorganization and procrastination can really hurt performance. As with all strategies, though, we need to evaluate these particular handicaps in terms of Mindy's goal, which is to reduce her anxiety by protecting her sense of self. She wants to avoid any situation that has the potential to unequivocally "prove" that she is incompetent, uncreative, or stupid, because her fear of that is the specific source of her anxiety.

Procrastination and disorganization provide a buffer between her performance and its implications for her sense of competence. However, that buffer requires that the corresponding attributions be less personally incriminating than they would be without those handicaps. In this respect, Mindy is treading a fine line; continued procrastination and disorganization are likely to lead others to consider her unreliable, unprofessional, and even lazy. Mindy may be able to maintain a belief that she is basically intelligent and creative in the face of those negative attributions, but she is unlikely to feel authentically and enduringly good about herself and her work.

Other costs to these handicaps are likely to appear over time, just as with other avoidance-based strategies. Continually mired in past-due projects and surrounded by chaos, Mindy is obviously not positioned to "seize the day" or take advantage of unexpected opportunities that might arise, nor is she likely to be able to go out and create those opportunities for herself. And it seems unlikely that she is ever able to actually *enjoy* the process of working.

Taking Cover

It may seem obvious from this analysis that Mindy's self-handicapping strategy has little to recommend it. As with Jeff's avoidance, its costs seem so clearly to outweigh its benefits that it is hard to understand how Mindy can fail to see that there must be better strategies out there. But Mindy has almost no experience working in a calm and organized manner, without procrastination—and it is of relatively little use to recognize that her tools are flawed when she has no alternatives readily available.

A SIMILAR SITUATION afflicts students and writers whose professors preach that they should construct careful outlines and rework their drafts. Students often respond to these exhortations by claiming that they "write better under pressure" and will actually do worse if they start working on a paper before the night it is due. Insofar as they have never done it before and thus do not really know how to construct a good outline or to edit their own work, they are right. Their initial efforts at such tasks are often disappointing compared to the caffeine- and adrenaline-fueled last-minute papers they have become experts at writing.

The first mistake in their reasoning is not in assuming that the papers they write under pressure are better than those resulting from their tentative first efforts using other methods but in assuming that the papers written under pressure are better than those they *could* write once they become more expert at those methods. The only way to learn this, of course, is to risk the failure and disappointment of working at something you have not yet mastered, and doing that requires—for someone like Mindy—being able to tolerate the corresponding anxiety.

People may also cling to less than perfect strategies because they are good enough to get the job done. One of the paradoxical effects of self-handicapping is that the relief from anxiety that comes from being able to point to a handicap to excuse poor performance may actually lead to better performance (which is then self-enhancing). Knowing she has a face-saving attribution at hand if she needs it, Mindy may relax enough to really pull out the stops. Given the potential for self-handicapping to relieve anxiety in the short term *and* the absence of a better alternative for managing anxiety, Mindy might actually be better off with her handicaps than without them.

Comparing the Tools

I argued in the beginning of the book that we shouldn't compare tools designed to do different jobs but that it would be helpful to compare tools designed for the same job. Jeff and Mindy have each developed distinct strategies—tools—for managing anxiety, and neither uses defensive pessimism like Katherine and Daniel. How do those tools stack up against one another?

Jeff attempts to manage his anxiety by avoiding the things that make him anxious, which works to the extent that he has fewer episodes of the acute, intense anxiety that precedes a particular event. Overall, though, he is still anxious most of the time, and he finds very little satisfaction in his life. He must be constantly alert to situations that might involve risk. As soon as he perceives that potential in a situation, he leaves.

This means that he is in constant transition, which in turn creates anxiety. Further, he can hardly know what he likes and what he doesn't, or what he might be good at, because he avoids situations that have the potential to provide him with that kind of clear feedback. He thus seems unlikely to develop a more consistent, positive self-concept, though he may well develop a consistent concept of himself as a "quitter."

Mindy actually seems to be doing pretty well in contrast to Jeff; at least she is doing the kind of work she wants to do and is reasonably successful at it. Despite the potential for paradoxical benefits from self-handicapping, it seems pretty clear that Mindy's strategy entails considerable costs. Although others may be impressed that she is able to pull off high-quality work, it is doubtful that her chronic lateness actually endears her to her coworkers, clients, and superiors. It also creates distance between Mindy and her friends because they cannot count on her, and she cannot spend as much time with them as she would like.

Although her handicaps manage her anxiety well enough to keep Mindy from running away from the situations that make her anxious, using self-handicapping as a strategy over the long term is likely to exacerbate her anxiety *and* to keep her from reaching her full potential. When things do not turn out well, she doesn't have clear feedback about why: Did her disorganization create the problem, or did she make some fundamental mistake in understanding the situation or formulating a response? Her handicaps are designed to make it difficult to make clear attributions for her performance; but to the extent that they work, they also make it harder to learn from experience, precisely because that experience is ambiguous due to the handicaps.

For Mindy, relying on self-handicaps means that she is unlikely to develop the confidence that comes from knowing precisely how to bring about a particular outcome. She may infer from her successes that she must be smart, but that inference is intrinsically different—less reliable—than experiencing the process of working her hardest toward a goal and knowing specifically how her actions contribute to outcomes. As long as she relies on her handicaps, she will never know how well she might be able to do without them, and this persistent uncertainty is likely to cause persistent anxiety.

Taking Cover

HEREDITY, TEMPERAMENT, and early experience all contribute to individual differences in people's typical levels of anxiety. Most of us are also more or less vulnerable to anxiety when feedback threatens our sense of self. People are generally motivated to maintain a concept of themselves that is both *consistent* and *positive;* when that concept is threatened, people feel anxious, and they develop strategies to deal with that anxiety.

Blatant failure, of course, can temporarily challenge even robustly positive self-images. But anxiety about our self-concept often arises from a more subtle threat, one that may even be present when objectively we succeed. For example, when we praise children in general terms for being good girls or good boys, without pointing to anything specific that they've done to earn our approval, we can make them anxious—how can they be sure we'll continue to think they are good if they don't know what they did to be good in the first place? (Some psychologists argue that this is exactly what we're doing when we comment on children's physical appearance, over which they typically feel—and have—no control. Sure we think they're beautiful and adorable now, but what if whatever made them that way today is gone tomorrow? Will our affection and care be gone too?)

Indiscriminately praising children with an automatic "good job" in response to every effort—no matter what its outcome—can also make them anxious. It tells kids that their performance is continually being evaluated, but they learn nothing about the basis of that evaluation. And as they begin to learn to evaluate their own performance (they can see that they didn't pick up all the Legos, so how can they have done a good job at cleanup?), our indiscriminate reactions come to represent an arbitrariness that, at best, is irrelevant and, at worst, frightening.

Our environment doesn't necessarily or always give us clear and consistent feedback about our abilities. When we don't see a connection between what we've done and our outcomes, we do not feel a sense of control or ownership of those outcomes. In psychological terms, this is called "non-contingent success": Positive outcomes are not seen as clearly and directly related to (contingent upon) our actions. When that happens, happiness and satisfaction with any particular success are short-lived and are quickly replaced by anxiety about what comes next.

Some people have a consistently negative self-view; their low self-esteem stems from firm beliefs that they are unworthy, incapable, or worse. Consistently negative self-concepts offer the cold solace of certainty and are associated with depression. Often, though, people who report low self-esteem are *uncertain* about themselves because they don't experience their outcomes as directly contingent on their behavior. They live with doubts about how talented, attractive, intelligent, or moral they are. When things go well, they feel temporarily more positive about themselves; yet because they're not sure *why* they succeeded, they don't know whether they will able to reproduce their success. ("Did she like me because of the way I looked, or because we had a good conversation, or because I make a lot of money?" "Why didn't he call? Did I do something to turn him off, or is he afraid of commitment, or have I just not given it enough time?")

Such uncertainty creates anxiety. Even worse, for people who suffer from deep uncertainty about themselves, each new situation can present the frightening possibility of *certainty* of incompetence. Uncertainty about how "good" you really are feels bad, but it may feel even more awful to know for sure that you are *not* good (smart, attractive, talented, etc.). For people with strong self-doubts, avoiding certainty because they fear that the news will be bad can be a strong motivation. One way to avoid this kind of negative certainty is to try to avoid any kind of conclusive feedback. If you never try, you never fail, and that philosophy forms the underlying premise of avoidance and self-handicapping strategies.

For Katherine and Daniel, defensive pessimism provides little attributional cushion for their self-esteem, nor does it shield them from their feelings of anxiety in the short term.

Their low expectations provide the consolation of having been right if things go wrong, but they don't remove the onus of responsibility from the self. Their mental rehearsal helps them to feel in control and to work hard toward their goals, but the downside of that process comes when they can't protect their self-esteem—by denying having had control—when things do not turn out well.

Yet despite their lack of self-esteem protection, the relative benefits of Katherine and Daniel's defensive pessimism stand out compared to the costs of avoidant strategies. The reward for being able to tolerate their anxiety in the short term includes increased chances of success in specific endeavors, greater long-term probability of a decrease in specific anxieties, *and* the opportunity to develop a knowledge of and confidence in their own skills and abilities.

Defensive pessimism focuses on *approaching* anxiety-provoking situations, not avoiding them. Katherine may not be smiling and whistling all of the time she is at work, but her defensive pessimism helps to ensure that she *is* actually working toward her goals, rather than trying to run away from her anxiety. Staying involved in the situations that make her anxious has clear payoffs: Not only does she accomplish a great deal, but each accomplishment reaffirms her knowledge that she is capable of working through most of the problems she confronts.

Taking Cover

As a result, over time, many of Katherine's specific anxieties have dissipated. She no longer worries extensively about *every* classroom lecture, because her successful past experiences have taught her that she can deliver a good lecture; her extensive mental rehearsals have also made her very aware of what she needs to do in order to give that good lecture (and to avoid various pitfalls along the way) and of the fact that she is *capable* of doing those things. She is far from becoming a Pollyanna, especially when it comes to her assessments of the potential for things to go wrong. She hasn't turned into an unanxious person, and she still relies heavily on defensive pessimism when she is anxious. Nevertheless, her confidence in her own ability to work hard and productively and to master the challenges she faces has increased significantly over the years. Most important, her strategy allows her to keep trying and to learn from her mistakes.

IN THE NEXT CHAPTER, I look more closely at how defensive pessimists are able to use their strategy on themselves to achieve personal growth. They are not uniformly positive about themselves any more than they are about anything else, but defensive pessimists are able to work through the negative and move toward the positive, even if the work-in-progress is themselves.

6

Negative Thinking Versus
Positive Illusions

Optimism doesn't wait on facts. It deals with prospects.
Pessimism is a waste of time.

—NORMAN COUSINS

Nothing is a waste of time if you use the experience
wisely.
—RODIN

I haven't come across a defensive pessimist who claims to
enjoy anxiety, but defensive pessimists do not tend to think
that their top priority should be getting rid of their negative
feelings—and they've convinced me that they're right.
Defensive pessimism involves learning to *tolerate* negative
emotions in order to get things done. Their tolerance isn't

passive wallowing in negative feelings; it embodies confronting those feelings and rejecting the premise that feeling good should always be our most immediate aim.

Empowering people to tolerate and accept negative feelings is a strength of defensive pessimism as a strategy and a capacity we may generally undervalue. It's also a capacity we can readily overlook, because it's upstaged by our visceral response to defensive pessimism in action. When we observe defensive pessimists, we often pick up on their anxiety. Then, our automatic reactions to negative emotions kick in, and what we're most aware of is that we want the defensive pessimist to feel better or go away (if only to prevent ourselves from "catching" their anxiety). We are convinced that the worst thing about defensive pessimism is the anxiety they live with during all that mental rehearsal.

In fact, being able to tolerate negative feelings can be crucial to a wide variety of life situations: delaying gratification, learning from bad experiences, truly hearing what other people have to say, and assessing our own circumstances, risks, and opportunities. If someone really wants to know why she didn't get the job she interviewed for—so she can do better next time—she has to be willing to endure the embarrassment and upset she's likely to feel when the interviewer explains that her sloppy attire created the impression that she was too unsophisticated for the position or that her rambling responses revealed that she couldn't think on her feet. No one enjoys that kind of criticism, and it takes a lot of self-control to handle it well, much less seek it out.

"Handling it well" means not getting depressed, not letting your self-concept collapse under the weight of criticism, and successfully figuring out how to use criticism for self-improvement. Copious research testifies to the arsenal of techniques that optimists employ to protect themselves from the negative impact of criticism, but, as usual, defensive pessimists do something different. But if they don't protect themselves as optimists do, are they putting themselves at risk for losing self-esteem and becoming depressed?

WHEN MY COLLEAGUES and I started doing research on defensive pessimism in the mid-1980s, research on optimism was expanding quickly, in part because of the explosion of attention to self-esteem. Literally thousands of studies by psychologists and other social scientists focus on self-esteem. In society-at-large, lack of self-esteem or poor self-image shoulder the blame for myriad personal and social problems: underachievement, depression, illiteracy, teenage pregnancy, drug use, domestic abuse, poverty. Correspondingly, a variety of social programs and self-help books aim to help people feel better about themselves.

More than coincidence connects research on various kinds of optimism with research on self-esteem; many of the benefits of positive thinking accrue specifically from positive thinking about the self. Several prominent researchers argue that protecting a positive self-concept is so important that *distorting reality* to maintain a positive self-concept may be the route to mental health. In fact, the most influential paper arguing this position claims that three illusions are helpful, and *perhaps even necessary,* to effective adaptation: an illusory sense of control, unrealistic optimism, and overly positive self-evaluations.

It would be bad news for defensive pessimists, who do not tend to indulge in these positive illusions, and whose self-concepts are not overly positive, if these illusions provided an exclusive route to mental health. To understand how the defensive pessimists' negative thinking is an alternative adaptive pathway, we need to examine the road not taken.

POSITIVE ILLUSIONS REVISITED

Illusory control is feeling in control even if objectively we're not, as when we'd rather pick our own lottery number or roll the dice for ourselves because that way we're in the driver's seat and can improve our chances of winning. (Our illusions can be so strong that we don't even understand why feeling in control when we pick our own lottery number is illusory—but it is.)

The Positive Power of Negative Thinking

Feeling in control increases motivation, even if we're really not in control, whereas feeling out of control, even when reality justifies that feeling, increases anxiety and leads to giving up. Given that trying usually leads to better outcomes than not trying, feeling in control typically relates to better outcomes than not feeling in control.

Similarly, having positive expectations, even if they are unrealistic, tends to increase motivation—and to lead to feeling more in control and in a better mood. Bill's expectations that he will do well make him feel good and help him to believe that his effort will pay off, so he is more likely to work hard, which increases his chances of doing well. (This may sound familiar as a description of a self-fulfilling prophecy.)

The positive mood benefits of optimism occur regardless of whether our expectations are realistic. If we expect to hear that our salary has been tripled at our next performance review, or we're sure that the doctor will report that we're magnificent physical specimens when we go in for our yearly exam, those expectations make us feel good, even though for most people they are highly unlikely to be fulfilled.

Even when it makes us feel good, though, unrealistic optimism carries risks. If Bill is too unrealistically optimistic, he may conclude that he does not have to work very hard—

surely something his clients won't appreciate. There are studies that show that unrealistic optimism is related to less adherence to medical regimes and less attention to safety and prevention; unrealistic optimists, for example, are more likely to abandon exercise programs because they're overly confident that they're healthy.

In part because he feels good about himself, Bill tends to feel good generally. Bolstered by his positive self-image and inclined to feel that failures are not his fault (which, in turn, further protects his self-image), he perseveres in the face of obstacles and setbacks. Positive expectations, positive self-evaluation, positive emotion, feelings of control, and motivation all interconnect in a virtuous, positive, self-perpetuating cycle. And the beneficial results from this positive cycle justify interpretations of the world in ways that protect and enhance the self, even if those interpretations distort reality.

So far, so good for strategic optimists. Strategic optimists have high self-esteem, and they avail themselves of positive illusions to support it whenever necessary. People who lack this positive sense of self—developed and maintained by positive illusions—are demonstrably vulnerable to depression, likely to use less effective coping strategies, and likely to suffer more from minor and major stressors. Where does that leave defensive pessimists?

Are Defensive Pessimists Defenseless?

What is the relationship between the defensive pessimists' strategy and their self-concept? Does defensive pessimism put the self at risk? Defensive pessimists think more negatively not just about the potential outcomes of situations but about themselves than strategic optimists do, and they tend *not* to use positive illusion to bolster their sense of self. Although defensive pessimists may be better off than other anxious people, is defensive pessimism a liability in the quest for a strong and positive self-image?

People like Daniel and Katherine make it hard to accept that just because people think negatively of themselves, there must be something fundamentally wrong. Daniel captured an extreme view of the resistance to this conclusion in a cranky tirade about the self-esteem movement in California: "Why should everyone feel so good about themselves? None of us is perfect, and there are a lot of smug, complacent people who could use a wake-up call. If all we see are the good things, how are we ever going to improve ourselves?"

Daniel isn't the only one who struggles with this idea that the only adaptive self-concept is an overwhelmingly positive one and that mildly distorting reality is the lowest-cost way to achieve it. Psychologists continue to debate—often intensely—what genuine self-esteem really is and whether and how it operates differently from the kind of positive self-

Negative Thinking Versus Positive Illusions

concept we can maintain with illusions and distortions. Where self-esteem comes from, what it is good for, how it may lead to good outcomes, and how to encourage it turn out to be more complicated than most magazine advice columns and talk shows would suggest.

Motivational speakers can put people in a better mood—make them feel better about themselves—with relative ease during an afternoon seminar. For $50 and a few hours of our time, we can let ourselves be caught up in the enthusiasm of a charismatic speaker and the promise of "Ten Easy Steps to Self-confidence"; we leave the hotel ballroom feeling energized and motivated. Most "quick-fix" approaches to self-esteem assume that the genuine article is no more than the rosy glow from positive feelings the speaker generated.

Unfortunately, a day or two later, we realize our lives (our selves) haven't significantly changed—the bills are still piled up, our boss is still a jerk, and we still can't wear size six jeans; the people around us don't seem to understand that they're supposed to see us differently now because we've had a transformative experience. With these realizations, the glow from our afternoon of epiphanies starts to fade, and there is seldom any lasting change in self-concept.

Similarly, some of the programs designed to build self-esteem in children consist primarily of telling kids that they are good people. Children should know that they are valued, especially by those who are central in their lives, and telling them is one way for them to know. There's a downside here though. Children, like adults, are semi-rational human beings, filled with curiosity about the world. Sooner or later they are going to ask, "How do they *know* I'm such a good (smart, valuable, competent) person?" They will want to understand (and agree with) the basis for the positive things they hear about themselves.

We tend to experience that kind of positive "valuing" from others, with no connection to anything that we are thinking or doing, as the kind of noncontingent reward discussed earlier (as a reward or consequence that is not under our control). Rather than building a strong sense of self-esteem, noncontingent reactions lead to excess reliance on others' opinions, or to devaluation of the person providing the evaluation ("little do they know"), and to increased uncertainty about one's self and the world.

To alleviate those doubts and to develop a consistent sense of self, individuals need to be able to explore their own talents and capacities, to experience trying, failing, and trying again, and to interpret the feedback from their environments with reasonable accuracy. This process is potentially risky and threatening, especially for those who start out with a greater tendency to be anxious. In order to embark upon it, one has to be able to face the risk. This risk generates the negative emotions that avoiders like Jeff can't tolerate, but defensive pessimists, like

Negative Thinking Versus Positive Illusions

Katherine and Daniel, can and typically do tolerate such emotions, in keeping with their more adaptive strategy.

Some people try, with varying success, to minimize the threat of getting feedback they can't handle by using the self-protecting and self-enhancing attributions I talked about in the last chapter. Self-handicappers, unsure because of their unstable sense of self, preemptively protect themselves by resorting to handicaps: Mindy can get herself to try only by making sure she's got a ready "out" if she fails.

Strategic optimists aggressively confront the risk, armed with confidence and self-concepts that help them to see the risk as minimal in the first place. Bill, with his default assumption that he can do whatever it takes, rarely considers the risk beforehand, but he can seize the opportunity to self-enhance whenever possible. And should actual experience threaten his positive self-views, he can defend himself by minimizing his attention to negative feedback or explaining it in ways that minimize its impact. ("So the client didn't like that presentation—what does he know? The important thing is that he was impressed by my motivation, and overall the meeting went very well".)

EXPLANATORY STYLES

Self-enhancement and self-protective strategies rely on the ambiguity and complexity of reality; they reflect the fact that how we *think* about the world, rather than how the world "really" is, can determine much of our behavior. Any number of things may contribute to a client's negative reactions to Bill's drawings: a fight with his wife the morning before a meeting, a belief that he'll get more careful work from Bill if he is demanding, truly bad taste, or the realization that his needs have changed. Of course, Bill's drawing also really could be inappropriate—he could have misunderstood what the client wanted—or it might even be technically bad or simply uncreative. Bill is unlikely to know about all the possible influences that contribute to a particular reaction, and no one follows us around to monitor our interpretations of the world for their accuracy and completeness; however, he can focus on the interpretations that serve him best (unless and until someone tries to call him on them). He won't feel bad or unmotivated if he is able to interpret the client's reaction in ways that have more positive implications for him, and reality typically gives him sufficient leeway for those interpretations.

In a similar vein, many psychologists approach management of threats by looking at the typical explanatory or attributional styles people develop, which I mentioned briefly before in the descriptions of different definitions of optimism and pessimism. They contend that we have consistent tendencies to understand and explain reality in particular ways and that these tendencies comprise personal styles that are fairly stable over time and constant across situations.

An *optimistic* and protective attributional style is a tendency to attribute bad things to factors that are external, unstable, and specific—as Mindy does when things go badly. The difference between Mindy's self-handicapping and an attributional style is that one can have an optimistic attributional style, as strategic optimists do, without setting up specific excuses before the fact, as self-handicappers do.

When something bad happens to us, the argument goes, we'll feel better, protect our self-concepts, and be more motivated in the future if we can tell ourselves that forces for which we were not responsible, that will change over time, and that only affect limited situations, caused that outcome. That way, we don't need to feel personally guilty or incompetent, nor do we need to worry that this one bad event will necessarily happen again and again or that our whole life is falling apart. If we attribute our loss on the tennis court to the lousy ankle wrap from the club trainer, we can maintain our belief that we're gifted natural athletes, and we can still confidently consider that we're debonair geniuses off the court.

Conversely, to capitalize on positive events (about which there has been much less research), we should attribute them to internal, stable, and global factors. We *won* our tennis match because of our intrinsic superiority, which permeates all the activities in which we take part, just as Bill "knows" that his firm is successful because he is brilliant.

Given that worldview, or more specifically, that self-view, why would anyone become depressed? And indeed, research shows that this optimistic attributional style protects people like Bill: When bad things happen, they are less likely to become depressed than people who have a pessimistic attributional style.

If we attribute negative events to internal, stable, and global causes and positive events to external, unstable, and specific causes, this *pessimistic* attributional style engenders a decidedly less positive view of the self and the world. Attributions about tennis probably don't lead to depression very often, but pessimistic attributional tendencies across more important events in our lives may very well do so. Convincing ourselves that our lover left because we are inherently unattractive, and that our promotion at work came only because no one truly qualified was available, leads to a pretty bleak picture of the future.

It's great for Bill, then, that he has an optimistic attributional style, but what does this mean for Katherine and Daniel? Defensive pessimists do not have this optimistic attributional style, any more than they rely on positive illusions to maintain their sense of self. If they don't take advantage of the protective cover for the self provided by optimistic attributions or positive illusions, does that mean they are doomed to a negative self-concept? Are they at risk for depression?

Studies show that the answer is no: They are not doomed to anything. *Defensive pessimists are different from other pessimists,* and they do not seem to be at risk for developing depression. Although they don't exhibit an optimistic attributional style, they also *do not* express the complementary *pessimistic* attributional style. Once again, they are different.

If defensive pessimists have neither an optimistic nor a pessimistic attributional style, does that mean that they don't make attributions? No—certainly Daniel and Katherine make attributions; their attributions just don't fit within the boundaries defined by the optimistic and pessimistic styles.

Research on defensive pessimists' self-concepts, self-esteem, attributions, and typical ways of coping converges on a much brighter self-portrait and long-term perspective for these negative thinkers. The process behind this surprising finding is fairly clear: Most of the positive effects of positive illusions follow from people actively taking control in their lives, and defensive pessimists do just that.

Recall Katherine preparing to submit a manuscript: She worries about which reviewers will be assigned to read her paper, and that is an issue outside of her control. But thinking about what reviewers might object to helps her to prepare the manuscript with extra thoroughness. She believes that if she works hard enough, she may be able to mitigate the effects of persnickety reviewers and still have *some* control over the final disposition of the paper.

If the editor rejects the manuscript, Katherine's attributions may include thinking that bad luck in the review process contributed, but she may also conclude that she didn't work quite hard enough. If the editor accepts the paper, she'll assume that the luck of the reviewer draw may have played a role, but so did her skill and effort. What will Katherine think, based on these attributions, the next time she prepares a manuscript? Her words: "The review process is crazy-making, and the only thing to do is respond by working like crazy." This approach is not exactly positive thinking, but it certainly is an activist stance.

LIKE KATHERINE, DEFENSIVE pessimists tend to make *complex* attributions about both positive and negative events, so that their attributions are hard to sum up as either consistently positive or negative (or internal or external, or stable or unstable). Playing through several possible outcomes before the fact contributes to their rich mental representation of *how* events can happen. When the anxious mother traveling with her toddlers thinks back on her trip, all the scenarios she rehearsed are packaged in with her other memories. They remind her that she was on target in packing the felt board and felt characters that occupied her kids for much of the flight; but they also remind her that she didn't get it right across the board because she didn't have the right snacks, which made for some uncomfortable moments (peanut butter sandwiches were too messy for that situation). She reviews both the good and the bad, and both influence her overall interpretation and attributions.

Defensive pessimists typically attribute both good and bad outcomes to *internal* causes, equally implicating effort (unstable) and ability (stable); but they also recognize that some tasks are very difficult and that sometimes the world is a tricky, unpredictable place. For defensive pessimists, these attributions imply that there may be every reason to feel anxious but that you need actively to take control of all of those things potentially under your control.

The pessimism of the pessimistic attributional style is very different. Attributions about past events have important implications for the future: Internal, stable, and global attributions for bad events lead people to feel helpless and hopeless, so that the prospect of taking control isn't even in the realm of what they think is possible. And that difference reinforces another distinction I made earlier: Defensive pessimism stems not from negative interpretations of *past* events but from anxiety about future events. Katherine's defensive pessimism doesn't stem from having had papers rejected in the past and being convinced that all her papers will always be rejected in the future;

rather, her defensive pessimism is a response to anxiety, which is rooted in an awareness that she is at least partly responsible for *both* her past failures and her past successes.

Defensive pessimists do not feel that everything is in their control—and part of their anxiety stems from feeling out of control. They feel, however, that they can take *enough* control to ensure that they can capitalize on whatever influence effort has over outcomes—and their strategy helps them to do just that.

HOPE

This ability to get themselves to work hard is fundamental to defensive pessimists' success, and it relates to another positive characteristic of defensive pessimists: Defensive pessimists, in contrast to other pessimists, have *hope*. Although common usage often suggests that hope and optimism are synonymous, in psychology they are distinct concepts. One prominent researcher has defined hope as the combination of *agency* and *pathways.*

High-hope people are those who can get themselves to act, which is agency, and have the ability to think of *pathways* toward their goals. Pathways thinking is very similar to the mental rehearsal defensive pessimists do, which increases the defensive pessimists' sense of their own agency. Katherine's belief that the answer to the world's craziness is for her to work like crazy is a perfect expression of agency; she doesn't feel in control of the whole world, but she does have control over her own actions, and she devotes herself to finding pathways toward what she wants.

TOLERATING NEGATIVE EMOTION

Assessing our own weaknesses generates the kind of negative emotion we find extremely difficult to tolerate, as testified by the creative self-deceptions we develop to hide our weaknesses from ourselves and others. Goals that focus on things we don't like about ourselves ("I have to lose weight because I'm too fat") are especially apt to discourage us, because every time we think of negative things about ourselves, we feel bad. When we feel bad, we are tempted to do things that make us feel better, without much thought for the long-term consequences, because it is difficult to tolerate feeling bad.

This process can quickly undermine our efforts to improve ourselves. We think of ourselves as fat, and we want to lose weight, but we feel bad when we think about being fat. One answer is to try to repress or deny that we are fat in the first place, which can be an effective self-deception if we are clever enough to avoid mirrors and the frank assessments of others. But it probably won't help us lose weight.

If we don't deny negative feelings, then we have to deal with them some other way. If eating ice cream has made us feel better in the past, we run to the freezer to make ourselves feel better, which of course only makes things worse in the long run. Our rational selves know that exercise is an effective way to lose weight, and once we get started, exercise— and the feeling of accomplishment that comes with completing it—can generate a positive mood that compensates for the negative feelings associated with thinking about being fat. But *starting* to exercise is just plain difficult or worse (nothing like latex to force those bulges into consciousness), which means we're stuck with those negative emotions in the short term. Being able to tolerate the negative emotion that results from becoming aware of negative things we want to change is crucial to our efforts to change them.

Defensive pessimism allows those using it to *tolerate* negative emotions as part of the process of working toward highly charged goals, without the need for self-deception. "Tolerating" negative emotion does not mean eliminating it, succumbing to it, or pretending it is positive emotion; it means simply allowing ourselves to experience our negative feelings, while getting on with what we want to do.

Defensive pessimists don't repress their anxiety; they fully experience it. Defensive pessimism may even exacerbate the immediate experience of anxiety when defensive pessimists begin to think about everything that could go wrong. The defensive pessimist trying to lose weight will cringe as she imagines the painful process of finding exercise clothes that fit, confronting the image of herself in the full-length mirrors that line the aerobics studio and the pain in her muscles the day after her first workout. Her detailed rehearsal then leads her to opt for unrevealing sweats, the opportunity to hide in a crowded midmorning class at the gym, and a schedule cleared to allow for a long soak in the hot tub after class. The most important part of her plan, of course, is that *it gets her to the gym.* Meanwhile, the self-handicappers will continue to find reasons that they are too busy to exercise, and the avoiders will bury themselves in soap-opera plots and wonder why their clothes keep shrinking in the wash.

Not in spite of, but because of their negative thinking, defensive pessimists get the same kinds of control and motivational benefits that strategic optimists get through self-protective and self-enhancing strategies. Defensive pessimists respond as flexibly and rebound as well after failure as strategic optimists, whereas those with pessimistic attributional styles, even if they make themselves try in the first place, are likely to give up as soon as they encounter obstacles.

A defensive pessimist who starts an exercise program will probably experience the same setbacks most people do: She'll skip a class occasionally and succumb to the lure of Ben & Jerry's. Other pessimists are apt to fall into "all or none" thinking and conclude that because they weren't able to abstain from ice cream completely, they're failures who might as well give up and eat the whole quart. The defensive pessimist, though, will be able to recognize that she's embarked on a difficult journey and that reaching her goals will require doubling her efforts. She'll throw away the rest of the Chunky Monkey carton and elaborate plans to make sure the freezer is stocked with no-fat frozen yogurt for the next time temptation occurs—her pessimism helps her realize that it surely will, and her mental rehearsal helps her to be ready for the battle when it does.

SETTING GOALS

When Daniel started college, he was anxious about the academic challenges he would face. He was even more anxious, however, about his social life. He flinched every time his first-year advisors and orientation leaders repeated their exhortations to freshmen: "All you have to do is get out there and meet people." "There are plenty of things to do and people to do them with once you get yourself out there."

He recalls how it seemed a little sadistic to keep encouraging him to get "out there," when, as he puts it, "'out there' was exactly what scared the hell out of me." Daniel was not at all confident that he would meet new friends simply by going out. He knew that he was not good at small talk, that he had a tendency to blush, stutter, and blank out with new acquaintances, and that he didn't have the kind of looks that would make him an instant magnet for social attention.

In making these self-assessments, Daniel did not conclude that he was an unworthy person or that pursuing a social life was a lost cause. What he did do, as a good defensive pessimist, was identify specific weaknesses so that he could rehearse alternative outcomes and develop effective plans.

Daniel didn't have fun cataloging his shortcomings and imagining embarrassing encounters. Worse, his roommate laughed at his problem solving, which included keeping breath mints in every jacket pocket, doing exercises designed to help control stuttering, and (nerdiest of all, according to his roommate) reviewing neatly penciled lists before going out on Saturday nights of hot topics in the news and questions to ask new acquaintances.

Nerdy or not, just as with taking a test or making a presentation, defensive pessimism helped Daniel manage his anxiety so that it did not interfere with his performance, which in this case was a social performance. Despite his roommate's ridicule, Daniel persisted in his preparations, and because of his preparations, he also persisted in going out, even though it made him anxious. Over time, Daniel met many people, several of whom became close friends. He suffered through his share of boring parties and disastrous dates, but also enjoyed his share of good times and romantic relationships.

The Positive Power of Negative Thinking

And his social confidence grew as he saw that he could meet new people and develop new relationships. His rehearsal did not turn him into a suave and at-ease man about town, and his friends continued their teasing every time they caught him preparing to go out to a party or on a date. But defensive pessimism let Daniel feel more in control, and feeling more in control helped him to take the initiative in talking to others. It also helped him to focus on other people instead of on his sweaty palms and the fear that he would say something silly.

Daniel's specific plans to cope with his anxiety about social situations are typical; most self-help books and social skills seminars provide similar techniques. Good advice isn't enough, however; it can help only if it is implemented. As a defensive pessimist, Daniel had the resources to actually carry through his plans, consistently, over time, even when they didn't yield fabulous results at first.

Anxious people who, unlike Daniel, have nothing but their attributions of terminal global failure to fall back on often stumble when they try to take advice about social behavior. They venture forth, bolstered by hastily overinflated confidence in, for example, "active listening," only to discover that it isn't easy to use that technique in a way that doesn't come across as condescending; sometimes people find it irritating and even react hostilely. Typically, a shy person responds to such a setback

Negative Thinking Versus Positive Illusions

with conventionally pessimistic attributions, interpreting it as confirmation of his unattractiveness, the insensitivity of the world, or the hopelessness of his situation, whereas Daniel used defensive pessimism to *anticipate* those failures and to put contingency plans in place to deal with them. Because he wasn't discouraged by initial failure, he was able to keep himself going until he improved enough that his actual experiences were more positive, even if they weren't entirely free of anxiety.

Daniel's experience using defensive pessimism as an avenue to personal growth is not unique. I've followed students while they're in college and as they make the transition to the larger world, having them fill out questionnaires periodically over several years to tell me about their experiences. This research shows that, like Daniel, socially anxious students who used defensive pessimism were able to form better social support networks during college than anxious students who didn't use defensive pessimism. By the time they were seniors, defensive pessimists had very close, supportive groups of friends whose intimacy and encouragement they could rely on and whose company they greatly enjoyed.

Like other anxious people, defensive pessimists typically begin college with lower levels of self-esteem than strategic optimists. Throughout their college years, however, they show a steady *increase* in their self-esteem. This increase in self-esteem is not incidental or random; they work hard to improve themselves. When asked about the things they are working toward, defensive pessimists tend to report more goals having to do with personal growth and change than their anxious classmates, and those goals emerge as more important to them than they are to strategic optimists. Most strikingly, defensive pessimists—like Daniel—experience substantial progress toward their goals over time.

FOLLOWING THROUGH

To put this research result in perspective, think about the number of times you or people you know have made New Year's resolutions that have been forgotten by Valentine's Day. Every year, around the beginning of January, you can bet that you'll see articles in newspapers and magazines that quote motivational experts describing how to set useful goals in ways that will increase your chances of making real progress. It is very easy to set goals, but much harder to follow through successfully. Expert advice on the hard part—following through—stems from a large research literature concerned with how people achieve their goals, and it boils down to three main recommendations: Make goals concrete and specific, rather than abstract and general; break large goals into smaller goals; and make an explicit, step-by-step plan for reaching each one.

You don't have to be a defensive pessimist to follow these guidelines, but note how closely defensive pessimism matches them. As defensive pessimists mentally rehearse various outcomes, they are turning abstract ideas into concrete and specific scenarios, broken down into different possible pathways, with elaboration of each particular step along the way. When Daniel wanted to improve his social life, he didn't just say to himself that his goal was to make friends. Instead, as part of imagining what could go wrong, he identified specific small goals: decrease stuttering so he wouldn't embarrass himself by speaking incoherently, keep breath fresh so as not to put people off, and maintain a repertoire of conversation topics so as not to look like an idiot with nothing to say.

These small goals are relatively easy to address with concrete action—even for someone who is anxious—and therein lies their beauty. Daniel's worries might have kept him hidden away in his dorm room, too intimidated to take action, if he had only defined his goal broadly and grandly ("make friends"). "Baby steps," like getting out the door to buy breath mints, make a giant difference, especially when we're anxious, if only because they move us toward, instead of away from our goals.

NEGATIVE SELF-KNOWLEDGE AND SELF-IMPROVEMENT

Small and specific also turn out to be the keys to understanding the negative parts of the defensive pessimists' self-concept.

Overall, defensive pessimists tend to score lower in self-esteem than strategic optimists (though they score higher than other anxious and pessimistic people). Rather than look just at the *amount* of self-esteem people report, however, my colleagues and I conducted several studies in which we asked people to tell us about the actual *content* of their beliefs about themselves.

Defensive pessimists do use some positive characteristics to describe themselves; their view of themselves is far from monolithically bleak and dark. Katherine knows, for example, that she is an innovative researcher and admirably thorough, as well as a loving wife and a dependable friend. Daniel knows that he has a good sense of humor and excellent problem-solving abilities when it comes to architectural design.

Defensive pessimists list more negative characteristics to describe themselves than strategic optimists, but the kinds of negative descriptions they generate also differ from those of other anxious people. When defensive pessimists describe their faults, they tend to be very specific and precise, in contrast to the more global or general descriptions of avoidant pessimists, for instance. Daniel might say that he has a tendency to stray from the point when he is writing and that he doesn't compliment his subordinates enough. Mindy, in contrast, will describe herself as a terrible writer and as too judgmental toward everyone.

Negative Thinking Versus Positive Illusions

Daniel and Mindy may both be right about themselves, and they may be very similar in these relatively negative characteristics. However, in the same way that more global attributions have different implications for the future than more specific attributions, the abstractness or concreteness of the way we think about ourselves has implications for how difficult or easy it will be to accomplish change. If you wake up in the morning thinking that you are lazy, then no matter how much you would like to change that, it isn't clear how you would start. What's the first step in becoming un-lazy? If, on the other hand, you think of yourself not as someone who is generally lazy, but instead as someone with a tendency to procrastinate, then that more concrete assessment leads more clearly to potential plans for tackling what is a much more manageable (though not necessarily simple) problem.

DEFENSIVE PESSIMISM AS SELF-THERAPY

In a very similar way, cognitive-behavioral therapists—who focus on how our thinking influences our feelings, motivation, and behavior—often urge their clients to make their negative self-perceptions explicit and specific and to avoid generalizing from one bad characteristic to their worth as a person. As an aid to attempts at self-change, this therapeutic or problem-solving technique follows from the assumption that fixing a problem requires clearly identifying it first. It isn't enough to know, for example, that a client feels he's a failure; it matters whether he's felt that way since childhood, whether it's a recent conclusion drawn from one or two events during which someone else was critical of his efforts, or whether he's lost six or seven jobs in a row and is on his third marriage. The therapist and client together need to figure out what specific events and assumptions have led to that conclusion and what kinds of events and patterns of thought would need to develop to alter that conclusion.

Problem specification not only helps us to formulate a plan, it also helps when it comes to evaluating our progress. The broader and more general the goal, the more ambiguous the potential feedback and the more room for individual twists of interpretation. Often that means that depressed or anxious people will focus on the most negative possible interpretation of their efforts to change, assume that one particular failure proves that they are a failure, or simply miss important feedback because they are distracted by their negative feelings.

When Mindy reiterates her perpetual goal of "becoming more organized," her progress is very hard to assess clearly. When she's in a good mood, she is likely to point proudly to her carefully alphabetized recipe file and to reassure herself that the rest of her life is soon to follow suit, even though she has no specific plans for what she'll do next. When she is in a bad mood, she finds little comfort in her recipes, because all she can think of is how they are the *only* thing organized in her life and how she only worked on them to avoid her other problems.

Setting more specific goals wouldn't solve all of Mindy's problems. If, however, instead of the broad (and intimidating) "getting organized," Mindy decided to "return all files to the cabinet as soon as she was finished with them" and "record every appointment in one place as soon as it was scheduled," then her progress or lack thereof would be easy to chart and much more difficult to distort.

THE CENTRAL FEATURES of the painstaking mental rehearsal that defensive pessimists use to approach performance situations also characterize their understanding of themselves. In fact, it seems that defensive pessimists use defensive pessimism *on* themselves: They see themselves in terms of very concrete problems that can interfere with accomplishing a goal, problems that may be surmountable with sufficient effort and planning. Daniel saw that he stuttered and knew that that might get in the way of making a positive impression on others. Stuttering is something that can often be overcome with enough diligent practice, so he set out to fix that problem, just as he tackles tough design problems in his work as an architect. In essence, defensive pessimists tend to view themselves as they view the world: Both are imperfect, have lots of potential, and are worth working to improve.

Defensive pessimists actually appear to have borrowed another technique that cognitive-behavioral therapists use with anxious clients: a "worst-case analysis," which is very similar in both form and function to the defensive pessimists' mental rehearsal.

When clients are anxious, cognitive-behavioral therapists encourage them to talk through all the bad things they think might happen. People who are terrified of public speaking may not have imagined specific outcomes. Instead, they may have simply carried with them strong anxiety, along with one monstrous image of a huge audience laughing and pointing at them, without any specific ideas of what could possibly lead to such a mortifying outcome.

Cognitive-behavioral therapists encourage these people to "concretize" their fears, that is, to try to construct detailed explanations of what they anticipate. Gently urging, they will try to get the client to describe whether he fears fumbling with his notes, or forgetting his speech, or tripping on his way to the podium. After eliciting specific events, the therapist will encourage the client to elaborate on what happens next: If you drop your notes, will someone laugh? Will everyone laugh? If they laugh, then what will happen?

These therapists find that playing through specific scenarios does for their clients what defensive pessimism does: It moves the focus of attention from feelings to the facts of the situation, allowing planning for and rehearsal of various contingencies. That increases feelings of control. Imagining the worst possible outcomes can also be motivating because one realizes that although the outcomes may be disappointing (or worse), they are nevertheless probably survivable (and often preferable to continued avoidance). It is unlikely, in other words, that giving a boring speech at a church fundraiser will lead to suicide, divorce, estrangement from one's family, or financial ruin.

Whose Reality Is It, Anyway?

Given that defensive pessimists do not use the same illusions to maintain their self-concept that strategic optimists do and that they are willing to acknowledge negative things about themselves, does it follow that defensive pessimists are more realistic? As is typical in discussions of reality, that question quickly drags one into debate about how to assess reality and accuracy. For the moment, lacking an absolute arbitrator for reality, it seems that both defensive pessimists and strategic optimists tend to distort reality, but in different ways. Each brand of distortion provides benefits but also leaves them vulnerable to particular kinds of mistakes and their consequences.

Defensive pessimists may diminish their enjoyment of life by continually interpreting the world in a negative way and potentially missing positive feedback and opportunities to feel good—a tendency that is both caused by and contributes to negative mood. Certainly Bill believes that Katherine makes much too much of every little mistake and that she would be less anxious if she could recognize how well she has done in her life. Katherine, of course, counters that she is less likely to make mistakes because of her careful consideration of possibilities beforehand, and she is willing to tolerate a little negative mood in exchange for feeling more in control.

Because defensive pessimists do not self-aggrandize as much as strategic optimists, they're more willing to recognize that they make mistakes, and by extension, they may be more open to learning from them. Daniel, after all, is the partner in the architectural firm who keeps the list of which clients have responded well to high-tech presentations and which prefer low-tech approaches. He keeps that list because he *notices* his clients' negative reactions when they occur during a presentation and is determined not to make the same mistake twice; he is often frustrated by Bill's apparent obliviousness to those signals. In contrast, Bill may have an inflated opinion of himself that leads him to miss some negative feedback, but that weakness may be compensated for by the positive impression his confidence conveys and by the undiluted motivation it provides him.

In the end, whether our perceptions and corresponding distortions of reality help us or hurt us is likely to depend on the *extent* of those distortions and the flexibility of our perspectives. It is easy to find examples of maladaptive perceptions: Gamblers lose fortunes and ruin lives because of unrealistic optimism and illusory feelings of control. On the other hand, when people feel extremely helpless, their perceptions of their lack of control are probably almost as unrealistic—and as maladaptive—as the reckless gambler's.

Defensive pessimists and strategic optimists both appear to *use* their slightly distorted perceptions of reality in ways that increase their motivation and lead to better performance. If people use their strategies in inappropriate ways or in inappropriate situations (without sensitivity to context), those distortions should fail to produce benefits, or bring costs that outweigh their benefits. Supervisors of nuclear power plants, we hope, will rein in their strategic optimism and err on the side of anticipating potential problems, whereas defensive pessimists need to resist the temptation of rehearsing a casual Sunday afternoon picnic, realizing that the worst that is likely to happen is that they'll miss the picnic if they spend too much time figuring out what could go wrong.

The Positive Power of Negative Thinking

RESEARCH THUS FAR supports this general picture of defensive pessimists' and strategic optimists' contrasting distortions and their consequences. In one study, my colleagues and I videotaped defensive pessimists and strategic optimists while they talked about the kinds of things other people would want to know about them, as if they were making a tape for a dating service. We figured that was a pretty surefire way to induce anxiety in those who were prone to it. We also told them that they would be observed from behind a one-way mirror and that two observers would rate the quality of their performance.

We had both strategic optimists and defensive pessimists rate their own performance. We then pretended to show each participant the ratings they received from the observers, but really everyone was shown the same two sets of ratings: One was relatively positive, and one was relatively negative. After a short break, we then asked the participants to recall as precisely as they could the feedback they had seen.

We could look at what the observers actually thought of both the defensive pessimists and strategic optimists as they watched them, and that gave us one measure of reality. Even if no one perceiver can be absolutely accurate or certain in his or her perceptions, some kind of reality is represented in the average of perceptions among people who are all observing the same thing.

Negative Thinking Versus Positive Illusions

We could then look at how each defensive pessimist and strategic optimist rated himself or herself compared to how others rated him/her. We found, on the one hand, that both defensive pessimists and strategic optimists agreed fairly well with the observers' evaluations of their performance while making the videotape, in that the same people the observers thought did well (or poorly) perceived themselves as doing well (or poorly).

On the other hand, even though there was relative accuracy in self-ratings, there was also significant—and different—bias. The strategic optimists consistently evaluated themselves more positively than the observers did, whereas the defensive pessimists consistently evaluated themselves more negatively than the observers did. Thus, both groups showed small distortions relative to the observer ratings, but in different directions.

The largest differences were in the ratings of how much improvement was needed: Defensive pessimists thought they needed to improve their self-presentation quite a bit, whereas the strategic optimists thought that they did not need to improve much at all. The observers, meanwhile, didn't see more need to improve for defensive pessimists than for strategic optimists, but they did see room for improvement in both groups.

Similarly, the defensive pessimists showed a consistent tendency to remember the feedback as more negative than it had actually been, whereas the strategic optimists showed a consistent tendency to remember the feedback as more positive than it had actually been. The defensive pessimists' and strategic optimists' memories in this study can be compared to an objective measure of reality, because they were all shown precisely the same ratings for the same amount of time, and we could compare what they remembered with what they were shown.

Neither strategic optimists nor defensive pessimists are completely divorced from reality, given the correlation between their self-ratings and the observer ratings. These results imply that the potential costs and benefits of defensive pessimism and strategic optimism are different, and it is fruitless to try to determine which strategy leads to more accurate perceptions of reality in some absolute sense.

Even if we could agree on criteria for such a judgment, it isn't clear that a comparison would be relevant to the real-life circumstances of those who use these strategies. To compare these strategies as if we could eventually declare a winner is to mistakenly assume that they are tools designed for the same job, when all the evidence shows that this is not the case.

The strategies we use in our lives are not randomly assigned to us. Instead, they develop as a response to the situations we face, which evolve in a reciprocal relationship with the rest of our personality, emotions, and memory. Different situations demand different approaches. Closer comparison of defensive pessimism and strategic optimism will clarify both the strengths and the vulnerabilities of each strategy.

People aren't blank slates. The strategies and sensibilities of defensive pessimists and strategic optimists cannot be interchanged or superimposed; they are a part of us and must be understood in the context of other aspects of our personalities. Defensive pessimists do not do well when they try to be more optimistic, nor do strategic optimists take well to the tactics of defensive pessimism. No one size fits all.

No Size Fits All

DIFFERENT FOLKS,
DIFFERENT STRATEGIES

No shoe exists that fits every man.

—CARL JUNG

The trouble with most people is that they think with their hopes or fears or wishes rather than with their minds.

—WILL DURANT

*C*omparing defensive pessimism to avoidant strategies like self-handicapping highlights some aspects of how it works, but we can get a better sense of the costs defensive pessimists may incur by comparing them to strategic optimists. Recall that strategic optimists, like Katherine's husband, Bill, typically are not anxious and have positive expectations. They distract themselves, rather than mentally rehearsing different outcomes, so that they don't become anxious. The differences in how defensive pessimists and strategic optimists think and feel demonstrate how strategies are integrally related to other aspects of personality.

Even in situations that typically make almost everyone anxious, strategic optimists are likely to feel less anxious than other people. Their strategy for controlling anxiety is to avert it altogether. In fact, the strategic optimists' strategy for dealing with impending performances or events is *not to think* about them. They are not entirely oblivious to the sorts of things that make many of us anxious; they understand that a course exam or a presentation in front of a new client or a "meet and greet" at a singles bar are all situations where they are likely to be evaluated by others and that all contain the potential for failure and humiliation. But strategic optimists typically believe they are in control, and they don't dwell on the possibility that things could go wrong. Their approach is to set high expectations and actively distract themselves from thinking about what comes next.

Bill, who occupies his time and his mind before a big presentation with e-mail, travel brochures, and the Nerf basketball hoop behind his office door, is a perfect example. He knows he needs to ignore the hassles and commotion around him if he is to be at his best during the presentation. Meanwhile, his defensive pessimist partner Daniel rushes about making extra copies of the handouts and organizing the backup slides in case the PowerPoint presentation fails to work.

When Bill's wife, Katherine, tries to get him to think about what will happen if they run into a traffic jam on the way to the airport and whether they should either cut out a couple of errands or allow an extra half hour, he's irritated because she is interfering with his strategy. If she is successful in her attempts to get him to think about what might go wrong, he may end up feeling anxious, which is precisely what he doesn't want.

NOT THINKING ABOUT something is harder than it sounds. To demonstrate this to yourself, sit there for a minute and try not to think of dancing white bears. Tell yourself firmly that under no circumstances are you going to let yourself imagine dancing white bears. Especially not dancing white bears wearing frilly pink tutus. Trying "not to think of X" *requires* that you think of X so that you know what it is that you are trying not to think about.

This kind of thinking is called "ironic processing." Research on ironic processes has a number of implications for our attempts to control our own behavior, thoughts, or feelings. It suggests that we might have more success sticking to diets if we focus on the healthy, low-calorie foods we want to eat, rather than on foods we are trying to avoid eating, because concentrating, for example, on "not having chocolate" means that we are always thinking about chocolate, which turns out to make it more likely that we will end up eventually succumbing to the desire to eat it.

Strategic optimists operate on a principle derived from ironic processing (though they probably aren't aware of that), which is that in order to effectively not think about one thing, you need to actively think about something else. They focus on distracting themselves from anxiety-arousing situations by thinking of other things. A strategic optimist facing an exam, instead of dwelling on what the grading curve will be like, how many questions she is likely to miss, and how likely it is that the optional reading will be helpful, will focus on how much fun she will have during break after exams are over, on how it would feel to lie on a beach and relax, or even on which of his collection of hideous ties her professor will wear during the test. Thinking about other things (typically, positive other things) helps the strategic optimist to avoid becoming anxious about what comes next.

STRATEGIES AND PERFORMANCE

Strategic optimists need their anxiety management strategy as much as the defensive pessimists need theirs. When, in our research, we interfered with people's strategies to see how they worked, the manipulations designed to influence whether and how participants thought about their upcoming performance affected the strategic optimists no less than the defensive pessimists. Defensive pessimists performed more poorly when we got them to do what strategic optimists do, but strategic optimists also performed more poorly when we got them to do what defensive pessimists usually do.

When we either distracted people or had them mentally rehearse their upcoming performance, strategic optimists performed more poorly and registered greater anxiety if they were prevented from using their usual strategies. And when we looked at the effects of different kinds of imagery on performance, strategic optimists performed best when they listened to a relaxation tape and much more poorly when they listened to a coping imagery tape.

Indeed, for strategic optimists, "positive thinking" proved to be just as disruptive as "negative thinking." Any kind of thinking is disruptive if our strategy relies on *not* thinking. Thus, Katherine's attempt to get Bill to think about some of the things that worry her is annoying to him not only because he does not like to think about that kind of thing, but also because it also may create real problems for his attempts at self-regulation.

No Size Fits All

In virtually every study I've done, I've found the same pattern: When the experimental manipulation requires that strategic optimists operate like defensive pessimists, they do badly, and when defensive pessimists are required to operate like strategic optimists, they do badly. These experimental manipulations create situations in which strategic optimism or defensive pessimism—depending on the particular manipulation—do not fit. Whenever their strategies don't fit the situation, defensive pessimists and strategic optimists find their performance disrupted. When they are in situations that *match* (or at least permit) their strategies, both do just fine.

MOOD AND MOTIVATION

Mirroring the research, Bill and Katherine differ in their typical strategies but not in their overall achievements, and both are highly successful. The same is true of Bill and Daniel, whose business partnership illustrates their totally different but equally effective approaches to a given project.

Most people, even in our achievement-oriented culture, believe that there are other important outcomes in life besides measurable professional success or school performance. Indeed, when asked about what they want most in life, many people report that they hope to be both healthy and wealthy, but they would settle for happiness. Being happy is one of the most important goals people have for their lives.

The Positive Power of Negative Thinking

Strategic optimists appear to have some advantage over defensive pessimists when it comes to happiness. Bill, for example, is often in a better mood than Katherine. People describe him with words like "even-tempered" and "unruffled," which no one would choose to describe Katherine. It clearly feels better not to be anxious than to be anxious. And if you do not become anxious in the first place, you do not have to come up with ways to keep anxiety from hurting your performance. Bill's strategy works well to keep him from becoming anxious, and avoiding anxiety helps to maintain his positive outlook and his generally positive mood.

Katherine, in contrast, often experiences negative moods. She doesn't usually erupt in anger, nor is she the kind of person who slumps around like a cartoon character with a black cloud perpetually hovering overhead (and it is important to note that she certainly does not suffer from depression). But, as we've already seen, she is anxious, and she sometimes seems less satisfied than Bill, even when things go well. Defensive pessimism makes her life work. Does she give up on it just because she continues to be anxious and is not as happy as many might think she is entitled to be?

Scores of studies document that optimism is related to being in a better mood and pessimism is related to being in a worse mood. Indeed, many people would scarcely need data from psychological studies in order to subscribe to the correlation: It seems almost self-evident. Yet, close examination actually reveals a number of questions that we need to ask about those relationships. Understanding how defensive pessimism, in particular, relates to important life outcomes depends on unpacking the complex interplay among mood, expectations, performance, and reaction for people who start with different predispositions.

Is Katherine's negative mood a *consequence* or a cause of her defensive pessimism? Just because we can see how Bill's strategic optimism may help him to maintain his positive mood does not mean that Katherine's defensive pessimism is responsible for her negative mood. It is vital to remember the fundamental point that Katherine starts out feeling anxious; anxiety has virtually always been a part of her life. Her defensive pessimism is a reaction to that anxiety, not the initial cause of it.

Anxiety is a big part of what researchers are measuring when they think they're measuring negative mood. There will almost always be a positive correlation between defensive pessimism (used by people who feel anxious) and negative mood (of which anxiety is a major component), because there is actual overlap in what is being measured. Indeed, if we "take out" the relationship between anxiety and defensive pessimism using statistical techniques, the resulting relationship between defensive pessimism and other kinds of negative emotions is usually greatly diminished or nonexistent. In other words, saying that defensive pessimists are in a more negative mood than strategic optimists doesn't really say anything more than that they are anxious.

MOOD, PERSONALITY, AND STRATEGIES

Temperamental predispositions are the foundation for more complex personality characteristics. They appear very early in infant behavior, they tend to influence reactions across a variety of situations, and they remain relatively stable across the life span. Emotionality is one of those predispositions, which serve as the building blocks for personality development. Infants who are high on emotionality tend to cry longer, more loudly, and more frequently than other infants. They are also more likely to grow up to be adults who have strong emotional reactions—the people who are always *very* upset, *furiously* angry, or *incredibly* depressed.

Psychologists now argue that two predispositions influence the structure of emotional experiences. One is the predisposition to experience *positive* mood, the other the predisposition to experience *negative* mood. People usually assume that the one is simply the opposite of the other—that the more positive you feel, the less negative you feel—but emotions are much more complicated than that. We can feel mixed emotions, such as happiness that we've won and sadness that someone else hasn't, or even conflicting emotions, such as simultaneous relief and regret when a challenging experience is over. Reflecting on our own complex emotional experiences enlightens us about the ways that positive and negative emotions are not mutually exclusive.

The theory that there are predispositions to experience positive and negative emotions suggests that from very early on some people will have stronger negative emotions in reaction to whatever they encounter, and some people will have stronger positive reactions to whatever they encounter. If positive and negative emotions really are somehow separate, some people may be high on *both* the predisposition to experience positive emotion *and* the predisposition to experience negative emotion, some people may be moderate or low on both, and some people may be high on one and low on the other.

Mounting evidence also suggests that there are underlying neurophysiological structures that relate to these emotional predispositions, as well as to an associated pair of motivational predispositions—the tendency to seek reward (an approach motivation) and the tendency to avoid threat or punishment (an avoidance motivation). Translating from the jargon, some people may be wired so that they find pleasurable things more pleasurable. You may be simply fond of chocolate and enjoy it when it's offered, but I crave it so much that I can't pass a candy shop without going in to buy a bar of semisweet. Similarly, some people may find unpleasant things more aversive. I dislike loud noises, but you find them intensely physically painful and will make every effort to avoid them.

Each of these motivational systems should influence the kinds of things we're moved to do and our personal experiences of different situations. People who are high on approach and low on avoidance are more likely to be big risk takers and adventure seekers: They pursue the excitement of skydiving or leveraged buyouts without much thought to the possibility that the parachute won't open or the market will crash. Conversely, people who are high in avoidance and low in approach will probably live fairly quiet, conservative lives because they're happier avoiding big risks and they don't find the big payoffs all that tantalizing.

A given person might have strong overall motivation, to both get good things and avoid bad things, which would probably mean his or her experience of life is pretty intense across the board. Another person may not be strongly motivated in either direction: Neither fear nor excitement moves that body off the couch easily.

The recurring theme of anxiety connects emotionality to defensive pessimism and strategic optimism. If different people are predisposed to experience different kinds of emotions with different intensities, then they will need to develop different strategies for managing their emotions. People who are high in the predisposition to experience negative emotion tend to feel more anxious than those who are low in that predisposition, and they may be especially sensitive to potential threat. That means that not only are they more anxious in situations that everyone would agree are potentially threatening (a job interview or a blind date), but they are also more likely to feel threatened in situations that others would find innocuous. For people who are sensitive to threat, a brainstorming session among coworkers or a friendly game of Trivial Pursuit at a party may feel like walking through a minefield, where every comment or answer has the potential to blow up in their face.

Defensive pessimists score higher than strategic optimists on measures of negative mood that are believed to tap into the predisposition to experience negative emotion, which makes sense given the strong role of anxiety in negative affect. In any objective situation, defensive pessimists are more likely to respond to whatever potential exists for negative emotion: They'll notice that their boss seems distracted and worry about what implications that has for how their team project is going, whereas the strategic optimist doesn't even notice the negative cues.

This sensitivity to negative cues precedes our strategies and is chronic and pervasive. The anxiety it produces is a genuine product of the way we're set up and is not something that is easily dispelled or dismissed by a change in perspective. That means that when defensive pessimists use their strategy, they do not feel un-anxious: They have not managed their anxiety away.

They do, however, successfully control it; they turn a potentially negative emotion into positive (effective and productive) motivation. To argue that their strategy can only be considered successful if they are able to feel as much positive affect and as little negative affect as strategic optimists is to forget that strategic optimists and defensive pessimists start from different places, with different tendencies.

Research suggests that defensive pessimists experience plenty of positive affect, that most of their higher negative affect relates to their anxiety, and that they let in a more varied repertoire of emotional experiences than strategic optimists. The variability in emotion they experience is consistent with the way their strategy unfolds: Their anxiety peaks as they anticipate negative possibilities and declines as they feel themselves taking control. Feeling bad and then feeling better must be more desirable that just continuing to feel bad.

Several times in interviews, defensive pessimists have responded with surprise to the question, "Are you unhappy?" They typically do not see any clear connection between their defensive pessimism and their overall happiness in life. They are amused or frustrated by the assumption that they must be unhappy just because they think about negative things. How can they *not* think about negative things, when clearly negative things might happen, and in Daniel's words, "it is my job to see that they don't"? From their perspective, it isn't thinking about negative things that makes them unhappy; feeling that they have no control over what might happen increases their anxiety—and that makes them unhappy.

The connection between positive mood and feeling in control—having a sense of personal agency—is almost as ubiquitous in psychological research as the connection between positive mood and optimism. Since the particular kind of negative thinking we call defensive pessimism is a pathway to more control, it has a paradoxically positive impact on the people who practice it.

THE PERILS OF POSITIVE MOOD

Thinking and feeling are intimately connected. Defensive pessimists can even be anxious about being in a positive mood because they sense that positive mood may interfere with their performance. Recall that in our studies, defensive pessimists' negative mood was positively related to their performance, and when we put them into a better mood, their performance suffered. Because positive mood can change the negative way they ordinarily think in the course of trying to manage their

The Positive Power of Negative Thinking

4

46

anxiety, imposing that mood on them, as we did experimentally, robs defensive pessimists of their strategy for seizing control of their feelings and, in turn, disrupts their performance.

Generally speaking, positive mood increases our tendencies to focus on the essence of a situation, without emphasis on the small stuff. Negative mood inclines us to more detail-oriented, painstaking thought. Research on creativity and mood confirms the stylistic differences: Positive mood increases creativity, *if* by creativity we mean the number of ideas people generate (or how quickly they generate them); negative mood increases creativity *if* by creativity we mean the number of workable, high-quality ideas.

Negative mood also affects our thinking because we use it as information: It serves as a cue that everything is not okay and that we need to keep working in order to make things better. When we feel bad, we devote time and energy to figuring out both what's making us feel bad *and* what we need to do about it, because we don't like feeling bad. Those feelings motivate us to sort through the piles of unfolded laundry to find a more comfortable pair of pants, or to figure out a way to change offices to get away from the coworker who drives us up the wall, or to add up our checkbook total yet again in hopes of finally having it come out right.

Negative mood can alert us to data from the environment and keep us in a problem-solving mode; it may also lead us to set higher standards for our own performance. That means we closely examine what's going on and keep chewing on things—a description tailor-made for defensive pessimists. As Bill says about Katherine, "She keeps troubleshooting, even when there's no trouble."

Positive mood provides information, too. Feeling happy is a signal that things are going along pretty well, and we may decide that we don't have to keep working or even paying attention. But when defensive pessimists feel happy, they're likely to stop thinking about what might go wrong—in other words, they stop using their strategy.

For defensive pessimists, being happy before a performance is a potential trap. Daniel's description of his reactions to encouragement ("cheerleading") from his family fits this pattern very well.

Being in a good mood motivates us to stay that way—but it doesn't necessarily make us un-anxious, because negative and positive moods are at least somewhat independent. Thus, defensive pessimists who feel happy can be simultaneously cheerful and anxious. Increasing their good mood doesn't eliminate the anxious part of the their negative mood. But because happiness increases arousal without neutralizing the effects of anxiety, adding happiness pushes them over their optimal level of arousal and makes it even harder for them to concentrate and prepare. That means that when the actual performance comes around, their anxiety returns to the fore, happiness notwithstanding, and their performance suffers.

For many of those using the defensive pessimist strategy, one or two experiences like Daniel's with negative fallout from being unprepared and "too happy" lead to an almost superstitious belief that being too positive can invite disaster—that it will cause the gods to strike us down for our hubris. This is the same kind of caution we express when we "knock wood" or admonish one another not to count our chickens too soon.

STRATEGIES, MOOD, AND MEMORY

Defensive pessimism and strategic optimism describe major differences in how people prepare for upcoming events. However, they are also associated with major differences in the way people interpret, react to, and remember what has happened to them. One of the things that Katherine simultaneously admires and finds annoying about Bill's approach to life is that he rarely seems upset with himself, even when things go wrong. When they did actually miss their flight to San Francisco—as she'd predicted they would—because traffic was backed up on the way to the airport, Katherine was biting her tongue lest she say, "I told you so," because she assumed that Bill would be kicking himself for not planning more carefully and leaving earlier. Then she realized that he had no inclination to blame himself for what had happened.

No Size Fits All

Bill was clearly not pleased about missing the plane, as evidenced by his enthusiastic cursing of other drivers and his impatience with the ticket agent. Still, after a few minutes he shrugged off the situation with a laughing reference to "Murphy dropping in" (as in Murphy's Law) and went back to the ticket counter to see about getting a later flight. He then reassured Katherine that he had saved the day because his persistence and persuasive abilities had gotten them seats on a flight that left only two hours later than their original reservation.

Bill's reaction to missing the plane is an excellent example of the strategic optimists' attributional pattern. Bill did not blame himself for not leaving earlier for the airport because he was not thinking about his own role in causing them to miss the plane. Instead, he attributed that bad outcome to "Murphy"—an allusion to forces beyond anyone's control. From Bill's perspective, even though he may be disappointed about missing his flight, there is no reason for him to feel bad *about himself.* Not only did he not feel bad, but Bill even turned missing the plane into a situation in which he could actually reinforce his positive feelings about himself: He focused on his successful efforts to get them out of their predicament.

However, when things go well, as on the occasions when he and his partner get a contract to design a new building,

Bill *does* make connections between his behavior and the outcomes he experiences. Bill contemplates with great satisfaction the effort and creativity he puts into their proposal and presentation to their clients. He revels in the validation of his intelligence, which he sees reflected in every new job they secure. In fact, even though he's quick to acknowledge that he and his partner work well together, he's thinking primarily of his own contributions whenever he thinks about the firm's success.

That attributional pattern can be instrumental in helping us feel good or avoid feeling bad. It also helps motivate us to pursue positive outcomes and gives us resilience in the face of negative events. Bill knows he is a talented architect, and he believes that is the chief reason he has been successful. Thus, when he begins a new project, he is confident that he will be able to execute it well because he will be able to bring to bear the same qualities that have led to success in the past. If and when he thinks about past projects that have not gone well, he sees them as having been caused by flukes or things that other people have done, and for him, they have no clear implications for what is likely to happen on new projects.

Katherine's attributions about the causes of her experiences are different from Bill's in ways that also have important implications for her experience, mood, and motivation. When things go well, Katherine, like Bill, will attribute her success to internal causes—her own ability and effort. Unlike Bill, however, she tends to think at least as much, if not more, about how hard she worked as about how able she is. (She often feels that luck has played a role, too.) After a success, Katherine is definitely happy and proud, but as she looks ahead, she cannot help but remember how hard she has had to work and how anxious she has been in the past.

When outcomes are not so good, Katherine's attributions also differ from Bill's. Rather than focusing mostly on external causes, Katherine maintains a belief in the role of internal factors. She may very well blame negative outcomes on her own lack of effort, even as she recognizes that other things may also have played a part: Despite the traffic, which she had anticipated, they could've made their flight if they'd gotten organized sooner.

Katherine, like most defensive pessimists, doesn't dwell on these kinds of thoughts, but they do influence how she remembers past experiences. Her memories then influence her as she anticipates new situations. Those memories include the anxiety that is an intrinsic part of her experience as well as her own efforts to manage that anxiety. Bill's view of the future is distinctly rose-colored at least in part because his interpretation of the past emphasizes what he has done well; Katherine's is less rosy because it is tempered by her experience of anxiety.

The Positive Power of Negative Thinking

BOTH THE RESEARCH results and the words of defensive pessimists themselves make clear that becoming more optimistic or more cheerful is not the simple solution to their problems that it seems. Strategic optimism may be a reasonable strategy for those who are already low in anxiety to use to keep themselves low in anxiety. But those who do not start out in the felicitous position of the typical strategic optimist—those who are, temperamentally or for situationally specific reasons, anxious even as they first begin to contemplate an upcoming event and sensitive to potential threat—need to manage that anxiety. Adopting the strategic optimist's approach simply doesn't work; and we can't wish our anxiety away. We may succeed in making ourselves feel better by daydreaming about being on the beach, but our anxiety will come flooding back once we actually have to perform, and things may even be worse than if we had not tried to distract ourselves in the first place.

Defensive pessimists need their strategy, and therefore they're vulnerable in situations where anything interferes with their anxiety management. If they don't have the time to engage in their extensive mental rehearsal, they might have trouble performing at their peak. On the chaotic floor of the stock exchange, for example, defensive pessimists would need to think on the spot, switching orders in midstream as danger loomed or opportunities arose—there wouldn't be time for

No Size Fits All

long, thoughtful rehearsal, and they might be vulnerable to anxiety in such a situation.

Defensive pessimists aren't the only ones who are potentially vulnerable in situations that don't match their strategy. Strategic optimists can also be unprotected. If they are forced to focus on what might go wrong—say their boss makes them troubleshoot in detail before submitting a proposal—their performance is also likely to suffer. Bad mood in general can tip the balance against them as well.

Thinking about situations that might make defensive pessimists and strategic optimists vulnerable also points us to situations where their particular strategies may be especially appropriate. Where careful attention to detail pays off, defensive pessimists may be right in their element. Where quickly grasping the gist is important, strategic optimists may do particularly well. Neither strategy necessarily destines people to live or work in only one kind of environment, of course, any more than any other personality predisposition does. Human beings are remarkable for their potential capacity to adapt and respond flexibly.

For example, in one study we gave defensive pessimists and strategic optimists sets of difficult situations (that came from the lives of other research participants) and had them generate potential solutions, which they told to an interviewer. Regardless of what each participant presented, the interviewer threw a curve in response, coming up with a reason the solutions wouldn't work, so the participant had to come back quickly with alternatives. Both groups responded pretty well to the need to react flexibly to something unexpected. In fact, it turned out that defensive pessimists' customary mental rehearsal prepared them to think very well on their feet; observers rated their responses more positively than those of the strategic optimists. (Maybe they would be fine on the stock market floor after all.) Other studies have found that both defensive pessimists and strategic optimists can adjust after failure—indicating that both can learn from experience and adapt accordingly.

Nevertheless, strategies stem from and are a part of the rest of personality. To understand how our strategies work and what they imply for our adjustment, we have to remember that they do not exist separately from the rest of us. They're tied to our different memories and to the different ways in which we experience the world.

As someone who is optimistic and not very reflective, Bill is disturbed by Katherine's pessimism and reflectivity. He sees his own optimistic outlook as completely justified by his success and Katherine's negative outlook as incompatible with hers. He believes not only that she is smart and capable but also that being smart and capable (with a judicious dose of effort) determines whether you succeed or fail. When

Katherine carries on about how anxious she is and what might go wrong, it seems utterly unnecessary to Bill.

From the outside, Bill cannot see how Katherine's defensive pessimism helps her to manage anxiety. Indeed, from his perspective, her negative thinking must just exacerbate her anxiety; to the extent that he perceives her low expectations and mental rehearsal as a strategy at all, he is convinced it's a defective one. He believes that she needs to calm down and that when she goes on about negative possibilities, it's just because she wants to be assured that everything is all right.

Katherine, for her part, has a hard time understanding what to her seems like Bill's obliviousness or denial. Her own experience makes it almost impossible for her to really believe that anyone who is remotely aware can remain un-anxious. Accordingly, she often presumes that he is either hiding his emotions or is outrageously insensitive to circumstances outside himself.

When we are with other people who use different strategies, the intimate connections among strategy, personality, and experience are not readily apparent. In general, we find it hard to believe that people who see things differently than we do are not wrong in some fundamental way, even though there are always aspects of other people's experience of the world that we cannot understand. When it comes to others' strategies, what stands out is the difference in viewpoint;

The Positive Power of Negative Thinking

what's harder to grasp is *why* they have a different viewpoint and what function it serves for them.

The next chapter moves from an examination of the implications of defensive pessimism and strategic optimism for individuals to their consequences—sometimes amusing and sometimes distressing—for relationships.

8

When Strategies Clash

SAME BOAT

DIFFERENT STROKES

Optimism is a force multiplier.

—COLIN POWELL

What passes for optimism is most often the effect of
an intellectual error.

—RAYMOND ARON

"Sometimes she ruins my fun," complained Bill. He was referring to Katherine, and his pithy lament summed up one of the
biggest risks of defensive pessimism: It can annoy other people.

Mood—both positive and negative—is contagious, and
our social norms favor optimism. Everyone knows that "Real

Americans" are extroverted, upbeat, and optimistic. Because we count on others to adhere to those norms, pessimism violates our expectations. We have to exert effort to ignore it or slow down to pay closer attention, and we can't proceed with business as usual in either case, which is irritating.

Social norms lead us to adopt the optimists' perspective on social interactions, thereby exposing the "transgressions" of pessimists. Social interactions involve more than one perspective, though, and we shouldn't forget that strategic optimists are not always ideal companions. Both Katherine and Daniel have been on the verge of strangling Bill any number of times, so there is plenty of irritation to go around.

Strategies clearly influence social relationships, and one way to examine their influence is to look at the social consequences their users experience. What kind of impression do they make on others? Do our reactions to defensive pessimists and strategic optimists depend on how long or in what contexts we've known them? Can defensive pessimists make friends and influence people?

First Impressions

Your mother was right: First impressions do matter. But there is no universal formula for how to make a good first impression because what is good will vary from situation to situation and from person to person. The guy who's an instant hit for his humor in the locker room may find that it makes a less favorable impression on his date's parents.

When we form first impressions of people, we are typically comparing the most salient things about them to our ideas of how people *should be* in a particular situation (in keeping with our own prototypes or stereotypes). Our impressions are likely to depend on whether we meet someone in a singles bar and are thinking in terms of potential romantic partners or we're interviewing potential baby-sitters for our kids. In these contexts, our desires and aversions will involve different characteristics, even if our images of ideal romantic partners and ideal baby-sitters overlap.

Generally speaking, strategic optimists make good first impressions, for a couple of reasons. They appear (and are) self-confident, positive, and in a good mood. In the absence of other information—which is the nature of first impressions by definition—we tend to believe what people tell us about themselves, and self-confidence is a powerful social signal. Unless we have a specific reason to suspect otherwise, we assume that the strategic optimists' self-confidence is a product of their competence. That, in turn, persuades us that their optimism is justified.

We usually respond to other people's positive moods by feeling more chipper ourselves. So not only do we like strategic optimists because we think they're competent, we also like them because they make us feel good. When people are around Bill, they find that their steps quicken and they are smiling more in response to his enthusiasm; it's hard *not* to respond that way and very easy to like Bill on first meeting him.

Dissecting the first impressions made by defensive pessimists is more complicated. Our response to defensive pessimists is likely to be a function of how much and at what point we first see their strategy in action. If we first see defensive pessimists while they are working to control their anxiety, our overwhelming impression may be that they are anxious and negative. A prospective client arriving early for a conference at Bill and Daniel's office might be disquieted, watching Daniel scurry around to double and triple check everything and overhearing predictions of disaster (though catching Bill shooting Nerf hoops might not really inspire confidence either).

Just as we assume the strategic optimists' positive expectations are justified, we're likely to assume the defensive pessimists' negative expectations are justified—that defensive pessimists are pessimistic because they've often failed in the past—and we're wary of them for that reason. As we interview doctors who may perform our elective surgery, and the defensive pessimists among them play through more negative prognoses than the others, we may believe that their negative expectations come from having botched similar operations in the past and that they must be less able surgeons.

Also, just as positive moods in other people can elicit a positive mood in us, defensive pessimists' anxiety and negativity may taint our interaction with them. Seeing someone else laughing can bring a smile to our faces, but seeing someone else's jitters can make us uneasy.

This negative reaction is not a foregone conclusion, however. Defensive pessimists are often able to project a confident, positive image to others. Both Daniel and Katherine successfully use their defensive pessimism to help them make a good impression in professional situations, where their extensive preparation bolsters their sense of control and mitigates their anxiety. By the time Katherine walks to the podium to give a talk, she looks calm and knows exactly what she's doing. In these situations, their strategies are not very visible; depending on the context, new acquaintances may not notice them at all.

When we filmed defensive pessimists and strategic optimists as they attempted to make a good first impression (the "dating tape" study in which we looked at memory for positive and negative feedback), people who watched the videotapes liked both groups equally well. The observers did not see the participants as they prepared for the videotape; they saw only the final product of that preparation. Since the defensive pessimists had their anxiety under control by the time they actually recorded their tape, it was not blatantly obvious to the observers.

The observers' impressions were based not only on seeing the embodiment of a strategy but also on seeing the whole person. For example, some of the defensive pessimists made jokes about feeling anxious, and the observers responded positively to that. Like those observers in our study, people outside the laboratory react to more than just our strategies. Strategies alone do not dictate the impressions we make. When we only *hear* about Daniel's blushing and stuttering, we may assume that there is nothing in his social presence that is positive. In person, however, as part of a whole package, Daniel's shyness and earnestness may well be endearing.

STRATEGIES AND ONGOING INTERACTIONS

Interestingly, even though strategic optimists tend to make good first impressions, those impressions may not hold up over the long haul. One of the most surprising recent research findings is that there is often a *negative* correlation between confidence and competence. That means that some of the people who are the most confident about their ability (and who may therefore make a positive first impression) are actually the *least* competent. We all know some variation of

The Positive Power of Negative Thinking

the brother-in-law who confidently assures us he can fix the backed up sink in fifteen minutes. Several hours later, our destroyed garbage disposal and a flooded kitchen suggest that perhaps we should have questioned his claim to expertise.

People who don't know what they're doing don't know what they're doing wrong and thus tend to overestimate their ability and become overconfident. Those who are most knowledgeable and skilled are aware of their weaknesses, and that awareness makes authentic confidence more nuanced. A truly competent plumber might not be so quick to assure us that he could handle our plugged up drain, because his experience has taught him that any number of problems may lurk under a sink of dirty water, some of which are easy to fix and some of which are considerably less tractable.

Even confidence that is initially unjustified can have significant payoffs, as when self-confident individuals are so strongly motivated to persevere in productive ways that they develop the expertise they lack. But to the extent that strategic optimists' confidence is not rooted in actual competence and that incompetence is revealed over time, other people may react with disillusion or disappointment in proportion to their high initial expectations.

This does not mean, of course, that all strategic optimists are unjustifiably overconfident or less competent than defensive pessimists. Bill, for example, really is a very good architect. (Nor, incidentally, does it imply that all defensive pessimists are competent; the strategy just lets whatever competence they possess manifest without interference from anxiety.) The message is, as your mother probably also told you, that first impressions can be deceiving—and that's true of the first impressions conveyed by defensive pessimists, too.

Defensive pessimists may contradict our first impressions by being either more competent than we assumed (if we first noticed their anxiety) or more anxious than we knew (if we first noticed their competence). Even if they initially presented themselves confidently, longer or more frequent interactions with defensive pessimists are almost certain to reveal their anxiety, especially as new situations arise. When Daniel presents a proposal to a new client, he exhibits both the building design and himself as products of extensive preparation. When he's chosen as the architect for a particular building, however, he enters into a very different kind of relationship with his clients—one in which they will have to confront problems together, overcome disagreements, negotiate compromises—and there he's sure to expose both his anxiety and his defensive pessimism because he will be using the latter (his tried-and-true approach) to control the former. But as Daniel works through his worst-case scenarios to come up with solutions to every problem he anticipates, his competence overshadows any doubts evoked by his negativity, and his clients usually react favorably.

SOCIAL INTERACTIONS ARE intrinsically fluid, despite the structures provided by conventions and social scripts. Recalling Daniel's anxiety about social interactions, and how he was able to make himself "get out there" when he was in college, reminds us that defensive pessimism increases our feelings of control. It helped Daniel to anticipate and plan for some of the expected give-and-take of conversation and to introduce himself in his most attractive light. It did not, however, transform him into someone at ease in every social interaction or enable him to make everyone else feel similarly comfortable. He still feels anxious, and he still relies on defensive pessimism to get him through new social encounters.

Nevertheless, several studies show that defensive pessimists can form close-knit, supportive networks of friends, just as Daniel has, and that they find those social networks more satisfying and supportive than other socially anxious people find theirs. My experience sampling studies (where participants report periodically during their daily lives) confirm that defensive pessimists spend ample time enjoying their romantic partners, friends, and family in a variety of social situations. Longitudinal studies, in which we have participants fill out

When Strategies Clash

167

extensive surveys every year or so for several years, reveal similar patterns and allow us to watch as our participants build their social worlds over time.

Defensive pessimists and their friends encourage each other, are emotionally intimate, and give each other material support and companionship. They generally experience somewhat different friendship dynamics from the ones that work for strategic optimists. As a rule, defensive pessimists have a smaller total number of friends but describe their friendships as closer and more intimate. The reason may be that when we get to know defensive pessimists, we become privy to their anxieties as we see their strategy in action. Knowing what goes on inside another person builds and enriches our relationships. For those who aren't initially put off by the defensive pessimists' negativity, being invited into their worries can lead to increased intimacy.

Strategic optimists ordinarily report a larger total number of friends and consider those friendships more casual and less intimate. Given that strategic optimists typically evoke positive initial reactions from others, they may be especially likely to have pleasant interactions even with people they don't know well. The generally positive tone of their commerce with other people may incline strategic optimists to classify even peripheral members of their social circle as friends rather than distinguishing some as "mere" acquaintances the way others would.

The Positive Power of Negative Thinking

To the extent that there is a bottom line in social relationships, here it is: Both defensive pessimists and strategic optimists are able to build satisfying relationships with other people. Although that is good news for both defensive pessimists and strategic optimists, there's still more to explore about their interactions. What about the dynamics of relationships with defensive pessimists? What is it like to love or work with or be the child of a defensive pessimist? Can defensive pessimists and strategic optimists get along? Do people work better with those who have similar strategies or with those who have complementary strategies?

DEFENSIVE PESSIMISTS
AND STRATEGIC OPTIMISTS: THE CLASH

Bill and Katherine have thought about, talked about, and fought about just these dynamics so much that they have developed a code word to describe the interplay of their strategies—The CLASH. Imagine that word surrounded by flashing neon lights, which is how they describe thinking about it. Bill's comment about Katherine ruining his fun provides some flavor of the nature of their clash.

Bill shares his view of a typical, frustrating interaction.

I come bounding downstairs after my workout on a beautiful Sunday afternoon. I suggest to Katherine that we drive downtown, check out the new exhibit at the museum, and then go to dinner at the restaurant that got such a great review in yesterday's paper. Before I've even finished talking, I can see the wheels in her head turning. Pretty soon the litany starts: "Where can we park? How likely is it that we'll get into the restaurant without a reservation? Will we be able to get back before Sarah gets home from her sleepover?" By the time she's done, my bubble has burst. All I wanted to do was go on a little Sunday outing, and she turns it into a major military campaign.

Meanwhile, Katherine begins to sputter, waiting to present her side of the story: She'll point out in detail why planning ahead beats worrying all afternoon and rushing through dinner. Bill will roll his eyes and grimace, and she'll stick out her lower lip in a classic pout. After a few seconds, though, they both start laughing, because they've been over this ground so often that each can take over the other's complaints. Katherine and Bill have come to terms, though it wasn't easy, with the chronic conflict between their strategies. They know that their strategies work well for them as individuals but can work against one another in their relationship. Knowing how the other's strategy works, and that they both need their particular strategies, has helped.

Katherine says, "Bill thinks that when I imagine what could go wrong, it's an accusation against him. Finding a potential problem with his plan means that I don't like his ideas or don't want to do what he wants to do." Bill counters that he recognizes that "Katherine isn't really being negative about me. Once she gets through all her worst-case stuff, she can have fun—and actually her attention to arrangements makes things go more smoothly."

Katherine matches Bill's generosity with her own:

I've realized that I don't really have to subject Bill to all the things running through my mind—especially not at first, or all at once. I do need to plan so that there's no disaster, but I don't necessarily have to voice every thought about every detail. Instead, I usually try to give him one or two tasks to manage so he can keep up his momentum. By the time we go, they're taken care of, and I've already started to relax.

A family therapist friend of mine reports that she regularly counsels couples whose strategies clash like Katherine and Bill. She finds that naming their strategies and explaining how they work can help break through the impasses that develop when conflict builds up over time. Being able to identify what is going on doesn't always make a situation less infuriating, but according to Bill, it keeps them from taking things so personally: "When I can say, 'Oh, that's Katherine doing her defensive pessimist routine,' I'm reminding myself that it's her way of dealing with things and not an indictment of me." Katherine also now understands that Bill isn't being oblivious on purpose: "He really doesn't have to get anxious, like I do. In fact, he hates anxiety, and that's exactly why my approach bugs him so much."

It's not so hard to identify other people's manifest emotions, but there are internal aspects of people's strategies that are much less obvious. In one study, for example, we found that classmates could quite accurately pick up the defensive pessimists' anxiety, but not their mental rehearsal. Similarly, in more intimate relationships, we hear some of what a defensive pessimist is thinking, but we don't experience the way negativity and mental rehearsal transforms his/her anxiety to produce a feeling of greater control. Bill hears Katherine's awful predictions, but he doesn't ask her how out of control she feels before she makes them compared to afterward, and he can't feel how her blood pressure actually falls during the process. How could he know that what seems so dire has such a paradoxical effect?

However, for Bill, and for my friend's clients, understanding the *function* of all that negativity can produce an "aha" experience: They suddenly catch on to what their partners are doing and why. They learn both to appreciate the benefits of defensive pessimism *and* to stand back and let the process unfold, without feeling that they have to "correct" their partner's negative perspective or "cure" their negative emotions.

The Positive Power of Negative Thinking

FOR DEFENSIVE PESSIMISTS, it can take one leap of faith to accept that strategic optimists don't share their anxiety, and another leap to accept that it is all right that they don't. They have to get beyond believing that it is their responsibility to explain to a strategic optimist just how dire things really are, so that he/she properly understands the situation and can respond appropriately. Likewise, once they can get past those obstacles, they can begin to understand that their negativity can have negative effects on others.

Daniel agrees that it helps a lot to understand that people start with different levels of anxiety and that they have different ways of approaching their goals. He remembers the teasing he used to endure in college: "Even though my friends would give me a hard time, after awhile they really did understand what I was doing and why. And I think that seeing me act like a klutz made them feel freer to admit that they felt anxious sometimes, too. Knowing one another so well—warts and all—made us secure and close."

Daniel still feels most comfortable around other defensive pessimists. With them, he doesn't have to explain why he's going through a worst-case analysis or try to hide that process. Just as important, other defensive pessimists usually don't try to cheer him up, which is a relief. "We do have to be careful, though," he laughs, "because sometimes we can end up freaking each other out by imagining more and more

When Strategies Clash

terrible scenarios, or we can get out of sync. One time I was just finishing the scale model for a design competition, and my friend Li Min came in. She started thinking out loud about a whole bunch of potential problems with the committee's response to the model, but it was way too late for me to do anything about it. Even though most of the things she came up with were too extreme to be very likely, I was a complete wreck throughout the competition."

Strategic optimists may find it stressful to be around defensive pessimists and more relaxing to spend time with nonanxious types with whom their strategies won't clash. Sometimes, though, different strategies can be complementary. It may not be a coincidence that both Bill's wife and his business partner are defensive pessimists. Over the years, Bill has come to appreciate their defensive pessimism as a useful brake on his own tendencies to get carried away. About work he says,

> I dive in headfirst and basically assume that I can handle whatever comes, and I like to think in terms of the "big picture." Dan sometimes seems like he's nitpicking, but I have to admit that he's helped us steer clear of some big blunders over the years. And the truth is, knowing that he's going to worry about things takes that responsibility off my shoulders. I can go ahead and do the things I'm best at—keeping the staff morale high, pitching to clients—while Dan takes

care of dotting my i's , crossing my t's, and basically covering my behind.

Daniel agrees that their strategies are complementary, but in keeping with his more reflective tendencies, he is also very aware of some of the potential pitfalls of his role in their working relationship. One drawback, for example, of being the person who brings up possible problems is the likelihood that you'll be appointed to solve the ones you identify. Other people may assume that the one who anticipates a problem has special insight into its solution, and that assumption can come across as a punishment for daring to be negative when everyone else is focusing on the positive. Daniel says, "You can't always be in the position of putting your finger in the dike to ward off disaster. In the first place, it isn't fair to have to carry more than your share of the workload. In the second place, it isn't really responsible to the organization. Everyone needs to be aware of potential problems."

Daniel echoes issues identified by other defensive pessimists when they talked to me about their strategy in the workplace. In particular, women defensive pessimists were very concerned that when they brought up negative scenarios, their anxiety and negativity—not the substance of their comments—would become the issue. Katherine notes, "People don't like to hear the negative, especially about their own ideas. If they can make it seem like your comments are just evidence that you're neurotic or a worrier, that makes them feel better. Women are supposed to be more emotional, so it is easier to dismiss their concerns." Other defensive pessimists worry that they won't be seen as "team players" if they voice their worst-case analyses, because bringing up negative possibilities can deflate the enthusiasm of a group that is excited about an idea.

One woman in a very prominent leadership role explained that she learned early on that the *results* of her mental rehearsal could win people over, but that she ought to keep the *process* to herself: Her rule is "don't 'do' defensive pessimism in public." She adds, "People tend to see anxiety and even a tendency to question or be reflective as signs of weakness and indecision. People want leaders who are confident, optimistic, and bold, and they want messages that are simple and direct. It's more inspiring." Research, as well as a casual look at leadership training manuals, supports her description. We do expect leaders to be confident and optimistic—indeed, those characteristics are on every top ten list of features that define a good leader.

In the United States, women, on average, report more anxiety than men and are more likely to be defensive pessimists (though there is much more variation among women and among men than differences between the two). It is difficult to tell whether women report more anxiety because they feel more of it or are just more likely to admit to having those feelings; the same is true for defensive pessimism. Even though we value self-confidence in both men and women, our gender stereotypes emphasize its importance more for men, who therefore may see defensive pessimism as an expression of lack of confidence and acknowledgment of defensive pessimism as an admission of weakness.

Women's traditional social roles may also have made it more likely that they will develop defensive pessimism as a strategy for managing their anxiety. With its emphasis on the details, defensive pessimism does represent a good fit for handling the conventional female responsibility for cleaning up after people—literally, as when we attend to our homes and families, and somewhat more figuratively as nurses or administrative assistants.

Women in previously nontraditional roles may find that their personal defensive pessimism conflicts with role demands for optimism and self-confidence. Yet despite the potential for conflict here, defensive pessimism may actually help them. "Defensive pessimism is indispensable for me," a successful corporate counsel comments, explaining that women leaders have less room to make mistakes than men in comparable positions. "I let other people think I'm optimistic, but in fact, I have to make extra-sure I've thought of everything that could possibly go wrong because I won't get cut any slack if I get overconfident and things backfire. When the pressure's on, defensive pessimism, however stressful, is my safety net."

IT ALSO ISN'T necessarily true that we should always hide defensive pessimism. One woman told me that she got promoted to her current position as vice president of a high-profile foundation precisely because she was willing to be the negative voice. In her previous post, she had served as an advisor to one of the organization's leaders who had learned the hard way to pay attention when she pointed out potential problems with new plans and projects. Even though he admits that he initially found her negativity off-putting, he became one of her biggest sponsors. He was the one who argued, when she came up for promotion, that the organization needed to hear a voice that would balance what he called the "mandatory optimism" of the workplace.

NEGOTIATING RELATIONSHIPS

Katherine, Daniel, and other defensive pessimists negotiate different solutions to the potential clash between their own preferred strategy and other people's expectations. Daniel and Bill normally split responsibilities in their firm so that Bill does more of the staff management and client "face work," capitalizing on his catalytic optimism and positive mood. Katherine, who has to lead graduate students and research assistants, has learned not to flood her team with the negative scenarios that rush through her mind. Instead, she'll work through them by herself. After she's had time to think, she'll gently bring up the negative possibilities she has imagined only if she continues to perceive them as likely enough to be of real concern. She's learned to try to pass on the benefits of her negative thinking without infecting others with her anxiety.

Many of our relationships are influenced by negotiations like those. Relationships between children and their parents, student and teachers, and employees and bosses all include some of the same dynamics. Especially when one person in a pair has authority over the other, the distinction between what we do privately in our heads and what we express aloud can have dramatic effects.

Modeling defensive pessimism for children who are anxious can be helpful—certainly more helpful than ignoring or ridiculing those feelings or trying to jolly them away. Talking through exactly what they imagine might happen can work for kids just as it does for adults; we can usually reassure them that the more fantastic things they imagine—all the "what-ifs"—either won't happen or will be handled by grown-ups ("I'll hold you up so you won't fall in the potty"). By eliciting their specific fears and rehearsing alternative actions with them, we can also help them learn to confront the situations that frighten them, increasing their sense of agency and ability to find pathways. In other words, we can give them hope.

As part of Career Day at my son's preschool, I once had to explain what I do to a group of five-year-olds (the only time I've ever envied firefighters). I resorted to show-and-tell. I gave them smiley-face or frowning-face stickers and told them a series of short stories describing various situations, such as "It is a cloudy day, and Mary is going to the park. What do you think will happen?" If the children thought it would rain, they put a frowning sticker on their papers, and if they thought it would get sunny, they put a smiling sticker on their papers. Each child counted up the number of smiling and frowning stickers they had used, and we talked about what it meant that some kids had more smiling stickers and some had more frowning stickers. The children were able to explain to me, as one boy did, that "it can be good to remember that it might rain, because then you will take your raincoat and boots, and you can stay outside and play. That makes Mary feel better about the clouds." Even at this young age, they could understand that there are benefits to entertaining negative thoughts.

Overtly expressing defensive pessimism *toward* children ("I'm worried that you will get lost or be kidnapped the first time you walk to school alone"), even in response to their ideas, is another story. If we relate our worst fears, we may simply frighten them further or make them feel discouraged, just as adults do if their ideas immediately and always elicit an extensive critique. Even though we can imagine all the reasons that building a fort in the living room isn't a good idea, our detailed descriptions of trampled carpets and tattered sofa cushions are more undermining than instructive.

THREATENED EGOTISM: THE DARK SIDE OF POSITIVE SELF-CONCEPTS

Defensive pessimists may need to tread lightly lest their negative thinking alienate, discourage, or depress those around them. Strategic optimists risk different kinds of fallout from their strategy.

Recall the self-enhancing and self-protective processes that strategic optimists typically use and defensive pessimists do not—claiming credit for success, while denying control over failure; being unrealistically optimistic; overemphasizing the importance of their contributions; ignoring or discounting criticism. Those processes help strategic optimists to maintain strong, positive self-concepts, which can be enormously motivating, as well as sources of emotional and even physical resilience. We seldom question either the wellspring or the value of high self-esteem.

When Strategies Clash

But an inflated or overly positive sense of self, one that relies too heavily on self-enhancement and self-protection, is fundamentally vulnerable to punctures from the outside world. This vulnerability goes beyond the pitfalls of simple overconfidence, which can be an error rather than a motivated bias. The more one's sense of self depends on positively distorting feedback from the environment—that is, the less connected to reality it is—the more potentially threatening *any* feedback becomes. All feedback has to be screened for possible negative content, and even positive feedback may not be positive enough to reinforce the shakily built self-structure. Not getting special treatment—the best table at a restaurant, the most praise from the boss—may feel like poor treatment.

People with big egos and thin skins, who are sometimes called narcissists, assume that everything revolves around them. Recent evidence suggests that people with such maladaptively puffed-up self-concepts are more likely to resort to aggression—and even violence—when their sense of self is threatened because they do not get their way. Even frustrations that most of us wouldn't take personally, as when the driver in front of us is slow to accelerate for a green light and we have to wait for the next one, may be seen by more narcissistic people as a personal affront. And even if they do not lose control, over time their exaggerated self-enhancing tendencies alienate their friends and scare off new acquaintances.

Strategic optimists are not all narcissists. Yet many psychologists have argued that milder versions of the positive illusions upon which narcissism depends are crucial to maintaining high self-esteem; if they use those techniques inflexibly or indiscriminately, strategic optimists—and their relationships—may be vulnerable to the same consequences narcissists experience. Defensive pessimists need to be sensitive to the risks of their strategy, but they do not seem vulnerable to this one.

Strategic optimists do more than just positively distort feedback (perceiving it as more positive than it is, selectively remembering only positive feedback, assuming that positive feedback is more important and valid than negative feedback). They also employ something called *downward social comparison:* They compare themselves to others who are worse off in order to make themselves feel better.

That may be a good emotion-management strategy—a good way to keep ourselves feeling upbeat—and it may contribute to the mood-related advantages strategic optimists have over defensive pessimists. It is less ideal, however, for our relationships in that it may lead to pity or even contempt for others. The general tendency to assume that we are above average implies that we consider ourselves better than most—not a flattering picture of other people, and not a great basis for forming relationships with them or forming unbiased opinions of their abilities or achievements.

When Strategies Clash

We may even maintain a positive self-image by actively derogating other people. Negative conceptions of others, formulated primarily to make ourselves look better by contrast, can then serve as justification for treating them badly, just as "in-groups" (junior high cliques, dominant social classes, established residents) typically do to "out-groups" (social misfits, ethnic minorities, new immigrants).

Fortunately for their families and friends, the positive biases strategic optimists award themselves are often extended to embrace their intimates, primarily because one of the ways someone can keep feeling good about herself is to appreciate how truly fabulous the people close to her are. After all, someone who has such exemplary friends and family must herself be pretty exceptional. And tacitly being dubbed great by extension may mitigate—for anyone close with an optimist—against the negative effects of egotism, since we almost automatically respond well to others who consider us special.

Yet even without derogation of others, the tendency to look at the big picture that is so characteristic of positive mood can cause optimists to construct overly schematic, stereotypic, or general impressions of other people. And given their tendency to avoid reflection, they are less likely to modify those quickly formed initial impressions over time.

In some cases, that kind of perspective can lead to relationships that have a generic quality. Optimists may spend little time or energy developing richly individuated conceptions of other people. Even if they treat other people in generally positive ways, they may not treat them as distinct individuals with particular tastes, desires, and feelings. Instead, they may immediately categorize new acquaintances and then treat them as almost interchangeable within a category. Think of the self-involved Lothario who assumes all woman will swoon with romantic delight when presented with a single red rose, or the cheerfully bustling aunt who buys identical sweaters for her three very different nephews.

We all do some version of categorization when we stereotype, and we all stereotype sometimes. But people who are strongly motivated to protect their own high self-esteem are more likely to engage in doing both, first because both support a positive self-image, and second because both are cognitively efficient, and that means there's more attention available for self-protection and self-enhancement.

Defensive pessimists operate differently. Their typical effortful thinking should help them modify and extend their initial first impressions and build a more complex and differentiated sense of the people around them. That doesn't mean that defensive pessimists are bound to like everyone they meet or to treat others uniformly well; defensive pessimists can be just as catty or mean as anyone else. In fact, they may

When Strategies Clash

be prone to weigh initial negative information about others more heavily than optimists do.

Examining how defensive pessimism and strategic optimism influence our perceptions of and actions toward other people reinforces the point that both strategies can influence relationships, and their influences *can be* negative as well as positive. These negative effects are by no means *necessary* consequences of either strategy, however. Awareness of differences in people's strategies may help us to be alert to and sensitive about the impact of our strategies on our relationships.

CULTURE, STRATEGIES, AND THE CLASH

Particular situations or contexts are likely to exacerbate or minimize the specific consequences of our strategies. America's strong heritage of individualism contributes to our emphasis on high self-esteem as an important individual value and to our endorsement of self-promotion and self-enhancement. The cultural value accorded to optimism and self-confidence may balance its social costs in the United States, and disdain for pessimism may increase its costs here.

Personal confidence and self-promotion are much less valued—indeed, they may be frowned upon—in many traditional Asian cultures. Compare the aphorism "the squeaky wheel gets the grease" to "the nail that sticks out gets pounded down." Differences in cultural emphases—or, as they have been aptly labeled, "cultural sensibilities"—suggest the potential for intercultural clashes in strategies. Imagine a stereotypically self-promoting American strategic optimist trying to work with a stereotypically self-effacing Asian defensive pessimist. The American optimist is frustrated that his hearty greeting doesn't elicit an equally enthusiastic response, that his vocal enthusiasm doesn't quickly translate into action, and that crowing about his accomplishments doesn't initiate a friendly and productive competition. He may even become worried that his new coworker, who readily expresses self-criticism, is clinically depressed.

The Asian pessimist may be offended by the American's emphasis on individual achievement over their joint enterprise, exhausted by the constant demand for cheerfulness, and suspicious of or confused by confidence that comes before accomplishment of their mutual tasks. At best, each worker finds the other's behavior puzzling; at worst, each may consider the other terribly inappropriate or even obstructionist.

Of course, not all cross-cultural pairings will resemble this exaggerated example, and cross-cultural clashes between strategies may become complementary in the same ways that Daniel and Bill's relationship is. Nevertheless, thinking about the stereotypes that correspond to different cultural sensibilities prompts us to review our typical assumptions. When they

When Strategies Clash

are braided into our psyches and our social conventions, those assumptions can determine the kinds of understanding and misunderstanding we experience in interpersonal relationships.

Given that strategies are related to other personality characteristics, is it really even possible to change them? If all strategies come with costs, what is gained by changing strategies? When is change desirable? What stands in the way of change, and what helps make it happen? The final chapter revisits the mosaic of costs and benefits associated with defensive pessimism across different kinds of situations.

Dark Side, Bright Side, My Side

PROSPECTS FOR CHANGE

I am just as little disposed to give way to undue pessimism as to undue and arrogant optimism. Both our virtues and defects should be taken into account.

—THEODORE ROOSEVELT

A man is a success if he gets up in the morning and gets to bed at night, and in between he does what he wants to do.

—BOB DYLAN

Mindy is struggling with the consequences of her self-handicapping strategy. Although it keeps her anxiety at bay enough for her to function—in ways that sometimes make her distinctly valuable at the office—her boss is frustrated that her work is almost always late (and sometimes sloppily done). Even though he admires her talent, he's hesitant to take the risk of promoting her. Meanwhile, Mindy's anxiety keeps tripping her up: Even when she vows to reform and tries to get organized, she's distracted, she forgets things, and she doesn't leave enough time to finish her projects. Should she be encouraged to try a more productive strategy for managing her anxiety? Specifically, should she try to become a defensive pessimist?

What about Jeff, the avoider? Should he either resign himself to an increasingly pathetic life, or maybe ask his doctor for one of the new anxiety-reducing drugs to help him face his fears? Or might he, too, be able to add defensive pessimism to his repertoire, as a strategy that would advance his life instead of protecting him from living it?

STRATEGY PERILS AND PROSPECTS

Defensive pessimism and strategic optimism develop in response to different experiences, and their strengths lie in the ways they address different problems. Defensive pessimism works to manage anxiety and help people feel more in control, whereas strategic optimism works to keep anxiety away and to protect self-esteem. In both cases, these strategies motivate effective action and often lead to good outcomes for those who use them.

Exaggerated strengths, however, can quickly become weaknesses. As we consider the strategies individuals use, we can see how both defensive pessimists and strategic optimists are vulnerable if they take their characteristic approaches to extremes.

Defensive pessimists could spend all of their time preparing, at very high cost, for highly improbable disasters; they could also become so perfectionist in their preparations that they never complete anything. Outfitting yourself for the possibility that you'll be stranded for days in a blizzard every time you leave the house is not a good use of time and energy. And if Katherine elaborates too many possible reactions to her manuscript—imagining each of her colleagues' particular objections—she may never be able finish it and actually send it in for review.

Strategic optimists may be so confident of their abilities that they persevere quixotically on impossible tasks, or they may be so motivated to avoid distressing information that they ignore real danger. Investors who are overly confident may fail to pick up on signals that the stock market is about to crash; indeed, the strategic optimists in one of our studies underestimated the riskiness of their sexual behavior, potentially exposing themselves and their partners to AIDS.

Dark Side, Bright Side, My Side

Costs may increase when we use our strategies in situations where they don't fit or if we're insensitive to their effects on other people. Strategic optimists who try to apply their strategy to get through an IRS audit may find that their big-picture processing doesn't mesh well with the IRS's focus on details. Defensive pessimists who trot out their worst-case analyses in a job interview will fail to dazzle potential employers. Each strategy may clash not just with another person's strategy but with a particular situational context.

RUN—HERE COME A DEFENSIVE PESSIMIST!

For defensive pessimists, many of the risks of their strategy come from its potential impact on other people. When I asked participants in my research to describe what they "feared becoming," defensive pessimists were more likely to list "boring" and "annoying" than were strategic optimists—and they hit the nail on the head in describing the downside of their strategy. As Bill made very clear, it can be a real drag to be around defensive pessimists as they play through their negative thinking out loud.

Also, other people may assume that defensive pessimists' negativity is *caused by* their strategy and encourage them to "lighten up"; that prompt, besides being emotionally exhausting, can actually interfere with their strategy execution.

Perhaps most costly of all, people may believe that defensive pessimists' negativity stems from realistic assessment of their competence and may conclude that they aren't up to challenging tasks.

In particular, their employees, students, or children may assume that defensive pessimists' negative thinking implies negative things about them. They may become discouraged because defensive pessimists characterize a certain goal in ways that are too daunting or because they infer that their own competence is being questioned. A child, hearing all the things that could go wrong in response to his offer to make dinner for his father may figure that Daddy thinks that he's just not clever enough to do something hard like cooking and may resolve not bring it up again.

If defensive pessimists are not sensitive to the effects of their negativity on other people, they may end up *creating* the interpersonal part of the negative scenarios they fear. Their bosses may not appreciate their strengths because negativity overwhelms everything else; subordinates may move away to avoid what seems like criticism directed at them.

All of these are serious consequences, but they are also only possible, not *necessary,* consequences. Fortunately for defensive pessimists, there is a relatively simple way to avert most of them: Don't "do" defensive pessimism out loud in front of other people. The primary purpose of the strategy is to gain control over private feelings, and there is no real reason that it cannot be done inside of one's head. The biggest risk of keeping your defensive pessimism private is that you will feel that others don't know the "real you"; but, of course, our strategies won't stay hidden from our intimates for long. And since intimacy also leads to greater knowledge of us as whole individuals, the risk that we'll be judged solely on the outward expression of our strategy is fairly negligible.

Defensive pessimists also risk getting carried away to the point that they use their strategy in situations where it is simply not worth it. Defensive pessimism does take energy, and it can temporarily exacerbate anxiety even as it helps us to control it. If we use defensive pessimism so automatically or habitually that we're rehearsing worst-case scenarios for an afternoon's worth of laundry or every three-sentence memo at work, we probably need to rethink our use of the strategy and try to develop less intense options.

CAN'T SEE THE FOREST FOR THE TREES

Anxious people are afraid of the forest, as a result of which they may never get close enough to worry about particular trees. Defensive pessimism helps them to approach the forest by getting them to focus on particular trees and move from tree to tree. Daniel did this by breaking down the frightening prospect of making friends into the unintimidating individual "trees" of stocking up on breath mints and conversation topics.

Ideally, and usually, defensive pessimists then move from their anxiety about the dangers posed by each individual tree to a feeling that they can in fact handle walking through the forest; even though they may occasionally trip over a branch or two, they also can enjoy the fresh air and exercise and successfully make their way out when they're done. After all, despite some bruising social encounters, Daniel now has a robust circle of close friends.

Defensive pessimists do, however, risk getting stuck in the forest if they can't make the transition from focusing on bad things that might happen to focusing on how to prevent those things from happening; they need to be able to look up and follow the path. They may also fail to see the beauty of the forest if all they think about and remember is their worry about tripping over branches.

If in dealing with our anxiety, we exhaust ourselves preparing for a blind date—exercising madly to fit into our sexiest clothes, cleaning the whole apartment just in case, running all over town to get tickets to the hottest show—we may end up falling asleep during the first act, thus defeating our own purpose.

The "expert" defensive pessimists we typically study—those who've spent the better part of their lives using the

Dark Side, Bright Side, My Side

strategy—don't fall into these traps. Someone unaccustomed to mental rehearsal, however, could find that getting into the specifics of negative potential outcomes is a peculiarly seductive process in and of itself. Returning to an earlier example, an anxious person who managed to convince himself that giving a boring speech at a church fundraiser really *would* lead to divorce, bankruptcy, and suicide has let his negative thinking run amok and needs to adjust his implementation of the strategy.

Novices may initially have trouble making the transition that ensures that, in addition to generating more and more scenarios of disaster, they include the "how to prevent them" part of the process in their thinking. If we take the worst-case instruction too literally, we may invent scenarios for which there is no effective preventive action other than avoiding the situation: If we convince ourselves that the auditorium roof really might fall on our heads smashing us and our audience to pieces, we won't be motivated to write a better speech.

The strategic value of negative thinking in defensive pessimism comes from using it *before* the situations that make us anxious. Negative thinking after those situations are over, however, quickly becomes unproductive rumination. When the purpose is no longer anxiety management, it's not useful to go over and over embarrassing dates or fumbled job interviews; when there's no proactive focus, negative rehearsal is simply depressing. Defensive pessimism relies on preemptive use of negative thinking, so it's important that those using it be able to turn off the negativity when it's done its job.

STRATEGIC OPTIMISTS: DO THEY EVER SEE PAST "ME" AND GET TO THE TREES?

In the short run, at least, strategic optimists don't encounter many social risks as a result of their strategy. Strategic optimism works well to maintain positive mood and self-confidence, both of which pave the way for pleasant and reinforcing social interactions. But strategic optimists can run into trouble if they find negative emotion so intolerable and negative information so threatening that they devote lots of energy to repressing it. Repression—keeping thoughts and feelings out of conscious awareness—has direct and deleterious long-term effects on both emotional and physical health. Research shows that those who deny their negative feelings are more likely to fall ill and take longer to recover from trauma and bereavement. Trying to maintain that we're unfazed after an earthquake has destroyed our home or our spouse has died takes a serious toll on our minds and our bodies.

The amount of distortion required to maintain denial over time can lead to interpersonal defensiveness—even aggression—and to inflexibility. If we try to confine the information we let in to only those things that conform to our inflated sense of self, we end up having to work hard to avoid people and situations that might force alternative conceptions on us, and we react badly if our blinders fail to keep out threatening information. Our social circle is apt to be small (and boring) if we only hang out with those who continually praise us and we strike out at anyone who dares to criticize us.

If strategic optimists defend themselves too zealously against negative feedback, they may miss or distort important information that could help them improve or keep them from repeating their mistakes. Remembering just your boss's compliment ("Good use of slides") after a presentation and discounting the criticism ("but your overall organization left something to be desired") may make your evening celebration more festive. But it won't do much for your next presentation—which probably won't profit from your ignoring the constructive criticism; and you may alienate your boss, who doesn't appreciate why you seem oblivious to her input.

Similarly, hearing just the "Thank-you honey" and failing to notice the disgusted look on your lover's face after he opens your present imperils both your prospects for the evening and the future of the relationship. Very few personal ads solicit significant others who are impervious, imperious, and insensitive.

Long-term relationships will certainly suffer if our self-image relies too heavily on self-enhancement and maintaining the belief that we're better than other people. Subordinates who have little choice but to put up with such attitudes may implement subtle sabotage against us. Or they may collaborate in our efforts to maintain our inflated self-views when they could be more productively spending their energy elsewhere. Those who have more freedom to decide whether to associate with us may very well decide it isn't worth it.

Even if strategic optimists are merely overly optimistic, as opposed to rigidly defensive, they may fail to take appropriate preventative measures, like the smokers who don't believe that they personally might become ill from smoking, the folks who build close to the sea despite the probability that they'll lose their houses during the next big nor'easter, or the computer owner who keeps no backups for the inevitable hard-drive crash.

Just as cheerful associates may pose a problem for defensive pessimists determined to focus on the negative, other people may interfere with the strategic optimist's focus on the positive. If your wife is with you when the doctor says you have to cut out high-fat foods and lose thirty pounds because your heart-attack risk is too high, she'll probably make it harder for you to recall *just* the part of the appointment

Dark Side, Bright Side, My Side

during which the doctor said your reflexes were still pretty good and your blood sugar was fine. (This is one of the reasons health care experts recommend taking someone with you for medical visits.)

In extreme cases, strategic optimists may be forced to keep others at a distance, because intimate contact carries the threat that the negative things we'd prefer not to know or to think about ourselves will be pointed out by others who know us well. Of course, this is also a potential problem for avoiders and self-handicappers such as Jeff and Mindy, who need to be wary of friends or family members who might destroy their protective cover by exposing their strategies and thus their fears.

Strategic optimists can avoid the risks presented by inappropriate use of their strategy if they remain flexible and moderate in the exercise of self-enhancing and self-protective processes and reasonably sensitive to feedback from others. In fact, research suggests that "expert" strategic optimists don't typically indulge in extreme distortion of feedback or treat other people badly. But there is a potential pitfall for strategic optimists attempting to remain flexible in their strategy use: They need to be sensitive to the situations where it's important for them to accurately interpret feedback or to respond in nondefensive ways, even if doing so makes them feel bad. That sensitivity, however, makes them more vulnerable to feeling anxious, and their strategy is not designed to help them manage their anxiety.

If they remain open enough to let in negative information, they may be open enough to let in anxiety, and then they may be vulnerable to a kind of disruption that they don't know how to handle. If our positive self-concept depends heavily on our belief that we're exemplary parents, letting ourselves see that we've been failing to connect well with our teenager may be extremely threatening; we may completely lose confidence in our judgment and feel helpless to develop new approaches.

CARICATURE, CHARACTER, AND STRATEGY

A review of the risks and benefits of these strategies makes it easy (and fun) to think about extreme caricatures of both defensive pessimists and strategic optimists. There's the out-of-control, detail-obsessed defensive pessimist who drives others to distraction with an endless frantic litany of "what-if" descriptions of disaster. This person ends up looking back on a life construed only in terms of narrow escapes and harrowing ordeals, where even success was always marred by intense apprehension and urgent, backbreaking preparation.

Meanwhile, repressed and narcissistic strategic optimists blithely bluster their way through every situation, occasionally raging at someone who dares to imply that they are less than perfect and wreaking havoc by acting without forethought. Looking back, they imagine a life filled with stellar accomplishment, tainted only by the failure of inferior others to properly acknowledge their obvious merits and by a curious lack of appropriately attentive friends and family.

While we're indulging, we might as well consider the positive extremes, too. There are the exquisitely thoughtful defensive pessimists, who—though cursed with an anxious temperament—rationally and methodically confront even the most horrific scenarios, nobly and modestly disdaining to sugarcoat the universe as they rely on honest hard work to both achieve a stable sense of self and save an oblivious world from otherwise certain disaster. Compare them with the brightly cheerful strategic optimists who insist on seeing only the good in themselves and others (for what is there to be gained from dwelling on the darkness?), and whose courage, confidence, and enthusiasm inspire everyone to overcome monumental obstacles and persevere even when all looks lost.

Fortunately, though we may meet one or two people who fit these extreme descriptions disturbingly well, living breathing people are rarely so easily reduced to cartoons. We're typically at least somewhat aware of what we're doing, and we're responsive to feedback about what's working and what's not.

The Positive Power of Negative Thinking

Defensive pessimists can turn off their strategy to go to the grocery store, so they don't end up always stocking provisions for enemy invasions every time they head out for a carton of milk. Strategic optimists can get themselves to pay attention to the world in ways that allow them to plan ahead and know that it's Aunt Ruth who loves steak and Uncle Fred who's a vegetarian, and that it's best not to assume that all elderly relatives are the same.

Since we often, like Katherine, use more than one strategy, it is especially unlikely that we'd resemble the cardboard figures just described. And their cartoonish one-dimensionality is even more obvious when we remember that anxiety isn't the only issue we confront in life. Certainly our repertoire of strategies extends beyond defensive pessimism and strategic optimism when we're thinking about how to raise our children, what kind of career we want to pursue, or what lifestyle would fulfill us. And when we choose a mate, no doubt we'll want to know more than whether a hot prospect is a defensive pessimist or a strategic optimist.

We are more than our strategies. Our strategies stem from and are embedded within the larger structure of our personality—our stable characteristics and dispositions, our self-concept, and our past memories and experiences. Temperament and heredity, our family environment, our childhood experiences outside the home, our choices as

Dark Side, Bright Side, My Side

adults, all influence the development and habitual use of strategies.

Nevertheless, our characters are also shaped over time by the strategies we use most frequently and reliably. Defensive pessimism is one strategic response to anxiety but not the only possible response. Once we start to use it, though, it influences our experience differently than, say, self-handicapping does, and we embark on different trajectories into the future. If we use defensive pessimism a lot over time, it becomes an important lens through which we see the world and an important part of how the world sees us. We become defensive pessimists or strategic optimists (or self-handicappers or avoiders) not by using a strategy once or twice, but by adopting it repeatedly and consistently.

What about the strategies-as-tools metaphor we've been playing with? Doesn't that imply that we can pick up and use any of a number of strategies as we want to or need to? Can defensive pessimists stop using defensive pessimism when they stop feeling anxious and out of control in a particular kind of situation? Now that Katherine feels more confident as a classroom teacher, does she forego her defensive pessimism in that arena and save herself a lot of time and trouble? Should strategic optimists adopt defensive pessimism if they find themselves in new situations that make them anxious? If Daniel were to leave the firm, could Bill compensate for the change by taking over Daniel's role as the one who worries? Would self-handicappers and avoiders be well advised to try to switch to defensive pessimism? Might Mindy learn to work on her projects long before they're due if she recognized her anxiety and harnessed it by using the defensive pessimist's techniques?

Theoretically and potentially, the answer is yes to all of the above. Strategies—especially compared to traits like extroversion/introversion—are relatively changeable. Rationally, we should change strategies, or drop current strategies, when we no longer need them or when they don't work well; likewise, we should be able to learn new strategies.

REMEMBER THAT UNDERSTANDING of defensive pessimism is informed by the techniques therapists use to help anxious clients and by the striking similarity between those techniques and the strategy. Cognitive-behavioral therapists find that they can actually teach their clients to recognize when their strategies are maladaptive and educate them about techniques like worst-case analyses to manage anxiety. They can also work with clients to help them discriminate more sensitively among different situations, so that they accurately pay attention to when different strategies are needed.

A cognitive-behavioral therapist would probably be able to help Mindy label her self-handicapping, for example; recognizing its function might reduce Mindy's need or even her capacity to keep using it to procrastinate and might open the door for her to learn new approaches—like defensive pessimism. That suggests that Katherine, Bill, Mindy, and Jeff may indeed be able to add new strategies to their repertoire and retire those that they no longer need, that are no longer appropriate, or that are too high-cost. Here, as in therapy, motivation, insight, the availability of alternatives, and the context surrounding their efforts are all likely to be crucial to their success.

The fact that these techniques are successfully used in a therapeutic context implies that strategy change is possible—after all, people usually go into therapy to change—and success with these techniques in therapy is impressive. But we also know from therapeutic contexts that there can be impressive obstacles to change. People often go to therapists because they don't know about different ways of approaching problems in their lives: We're not issued a how-to manual with possible strategies for all occasions at birth. And as convenient as that would be, even that would not ensure that people would be able to choose and implement the best strategies for them. To work well, strategies have to fit individuals as well as situations.

Other processes collude to make strategy change more complicated than switching from a hammer to a screwdriver.

Defensive pessimists may be motivated to cling to their strategy long after they've ceased to be acutely anxious in a particular situation because of an almost superstitious belief that positive thinking will surely backfire—as if they'll be jinxed if they dare to give up the ritual of negative thinking. Fear of being "too cocky" comes up a lot when defensive pessimists talk. Their fears may be partly justified in that any strategy change will require discarding old habits and learning new ones, a process that is bound to be disconcerting and disruptive. If they want to change their strategy because they are no longer so anxious in a particular situation, defensive pessimists will probably have to contend with anxiety about adopting a new strategy; that anxiety—though from a different source—may be just as debilitating as the performance anxiety they have outgrown.

Switching *to* defensive pessimism may present similar obstacles. Self-handicappers who attempt to emulate the defensive pessimists' productive kind of negative thinking may find themselves flooded with anxiety for which they are unprepared. Certainly the experimental evidence strongly suggests that imposing an alternative strategy on those who do not typically use it is likely to lead to problems, at least initially. Cognitive-behavioral therapists typically assign homework and emphasize the importance of practicing new strategies; they also provide detailed feedback on novice attempts.

Supervision like that facilitates change, but it may be difficult for us to duplicate ourselves.

This is one of the rationales for using drug treatments for anxious patients. If drugs can relieve anxiety directly, then patients have breathing space in which to learn new behaviors and adapt their beliefs about themselves, without the debilitation of anxiety. The drawback of relying solely on drug treatments for anxiety is that patients calmed by medication are not learning how to deal with the anxious feelings that may return when they discontinue it. The hope, of course, is that over time more effective behavior and a history of more positive experiences will decrease anxiety to less problematic levels, at which point the patient would be ready to control anxiety strategically, without the drug.

Even with medication or therapy (or both), we know that we can't expect to live free from anxiety—even if we're working to reduce how often and how much we experience, or even if we don't typically feel it much relative to other people. That's why developing and refining strategies for managing that anxiety matters enough to devote a book to defensive pessimism.

Discussion of strategy change obviously implies that there are times when we should *want* to change our strategies. But getting people to recognize that there are problems with their typical strategy in the first place may be one of the biggest obstacles to change. Mindy and Jeff don't really see themselves as I've described them—chiefly in terms of their strategies. (That's one of the reasons the do-it-yourself quiz to identify strategies is included in the book.) And of course, the whole case for defensive pessimism is that defensive pessimists have a perfectly good strategy, thank you very much, and they usually don't *need* to change it. The same is true of strategic optimists, albeit for different reasons.

Even if there is a good reason for changing strategies—which can only be determined by people reviewing their goals and the costs and benefits of their current strategies—it takes determination to weather the transition period. To throw another wrench into the works (and at the risk of confusing the toolbox metaphor), other people may be disconcerted by our efforts to change. We are comfortable to be around (regardless of whether we are likable or effective) as long as we're predictable—as long as we use our standard strategies.

Even if we're ready to change, then, those around us may resist our efforts by treating us as if we were still operating the old way. If Mindy suddenly starts mentally rehearsing all the ways she might lose out on a promotion, her friends are apt to be baffled. As they listen to the anxiety pouring out of a more negative Mindy—even if she does start organizing her portfolio well in advance of her review and making sure that her next presentation is neatly and clearly done—it might not seem like a clear improvement to them, especially not right away. And her boss might not be supportive either, especially if she messes up even more while she's learning to tolerate her anxiety well enough to use defensive pessimism effectively.

In spite of the obstacles to strategy change and in view of the fact that it's by no means always necessary or desirable, there are identifiable contexts where it's most likely to happen. Therapy is the most obvious context for strategy change, and one that underscores the role of motivation, insight, and supportive others in facilitating change for those who pursue it. We are also likely to see strategy change if we follow people through major life transitions, where they have to adjust to new situations, tasks, and people. Recall the anxious traveling mother who discovered that she felt unnervingly out of control with the advent of her children and "converted" to defensive pessimism to restore her capacity to take charge.

Defensive pessimists do tend to use their defensive pessimism less as they gain more control in new situations. A study designed to assess just that had students report about their strategies and feelings of control in their first year of college, periodically throughout their college years, and again during their first year after graduation; they clung to their typical strategies more tightly through the early months of their transitions than they did later on after they'd gotten used to a new environment.

In another study, those who moved into an environment where they felt more in control reported less defensive pessimism than they had previously, and those who moved into an environment where they felt less in control reported more defensive pessimism. These results do ratify the toolbox metaphor because these students didn't seem to discard defensive pessimism; rather, they seemed to have put it away so that it was still accessible if they needed it again.

OTHER PEOPLE CAN have major effects on our strategies beyond just reacting to them. Research on family environments indicates that they ordinarily work to exaggerate differences among siblings within the context of the family, even while heredity and other common influences lead siblings to resemble each other when appraised outside the family. For example, parents are likely to emphasize the differences between two brothers while they are at home: One becomes the academic achiever, the other becomes the social star. Their differences are likely to loom much larger when the brothers are with other family members (where each plays his assigned role) than when they are with their friends (where they are presumably freer to play whatever role they desire). Both brothers may be highly social, in fact, but that only becomes apparent in the context of their relationships outside of the family.

Our strategies can be directly influenced by such dynamics. If the role of the strategic optimist or defensive pessimist is already taken by the time we arrive on the family scene, we may adopt a contrasting strategy by default—at least while we're in the bosom of our families. Even when two children have temperamentally comparable tendencies to be anxious, if the older sister develops defensive pessimism ("the careful one"), parents' assumptions that the younger sister will be different may push her into developing a different strategy, such as self-handicapping ("the irresponsible one").

The child who uses self-handicapping while at home in response to her parents' expectations that she be different from a sibling may develop defensive pessimism as she becomes more self-sufficient away from home. Indeed, the question of who—among those who are anxious—is likely to develop defensive pessimism is a prime avenue for further research. Older children, who may be more likely to develop it initially in response to anxiety induced by their parents' higher expectations and greater scrutiny, may relax as they gain independence and no longer need their defensive pessimism. As we move into different roles, our experiences, responsibilities, and resources change, and consequently our anxiety levels may change. Our strategies may well change with them.

The Positive Power of Negative Thinking

Thus, people vary in the extent to which they use each strategy, according to the relationships they're in—and that's illustrated most clearly when we consider the strategic optimist/defensive pessimist pairing. Notice that with Daniel in the role of defensive pessimist, Bill can give full rein to his optimism; if Daniel were also a strategic optimist, Bill might have to modify his own strategy to make sure that the partnership as a whole functioned optimally.

Similar dynamics obtain in Bill's relationship with Katherine. For instance, she—in a rather striking contrast to her behavior in other domains—is so generally unconcerned about money and so confident of Bill's expertise in that department that she actually behaves like a strategic optimist in money matters: She doesn't sweat the details, feels securely that everything is fine, and seems a little unrealistic about her own spending habits. For his part, Bill becomes something of a defensive pessimist when he's dealing with his daughter, who he claims doesn't understand the accidents just waiting to happen to her if she's not super-careful; he becomes super-careful on her behalf (whether she likes it or not). Her resentment of his vigilance, in turn, makes it likely that she will adopt an infuriatingly opposite strategy, becoming less like a defensive pessimist and even more like the oblivious optimist he fears she is.

We can and do adapt to the strengths, weaknesses, needs, and desires of other people—as they do to ours, so we

Dark Side, Bright Side, My Side

shouldn't be too surprised to find that we're able to call on different strategies as we move from domain to domain within relationships, and from relationship to relationship.

THE POSITIVE POWER
OF NEGATIVE THINKING

An interviewer once asked me if I thought our society's treatment of pessimism was similar to the ways we used to treat left-handers, and that was an excellent analogy in many ways. Just like handedness in the past, pessimism and optimism, currently and historically, readily take on moral connotations. Pessimism is sinister compared to the wholesome simplicity of optimism; it reflects a suspicious lack of faith.

As a result of misguided assumptions about handedness, teachers and parents engaged for years in extensive, damaging, and largely unfruitful efforts to get left-handed children to switch their dominant hand. We're more enlightened on this issue now. Left-handers probably still have a hard time in a world largely set up for right-handers, but we now know that trying to change handedness doesn't work *and* isn't necessary: Left-handers are able to do pretty much everything right-handers can do; they just do it differently. Acceptance of left-handers in no way implies rejection or denigration of right-handers—even if it leaves exposed some of our erroneous previous assumptions.

Likewise, arguing *for* negative thinking under certain circumstances is very different from arguing *against* positive thinking. Defensive pessimists do things differently, too—even if things are sometimes harder for them than for strategic optimists, they're fully able to do what they set out to do. They do not need to be cured of their defensive pessimism; indeed, defensive pessimism is already the treatment for the anxiety that ails them.

References

The following are good readable introductions to different kinds of optimism and pessimism and related concepts covered in this book.

Baumeister, R. F., B. J. Bushman, and W. K. Campbell. 2000. Self-esteem, narcissism, and aggression: Does violence result from low self-esteem or from threatened egotism? *Current Directions in Psychological Science* 9 (1): 26–29.

Held, B. 2001. *Stop Smiling, Start Kvetching: A Five-Step Guide to Creative Complaining.* New York: St. Martin's Press.

Pennebaker, J. W. 1997. *Opening Up: The Healing Power of Expressing Emotions,* rev. ed. New York: Guilford Press.

Peterson, C., and L. M. Bossio. 1991. *Health and Optimism.* New York: Free Press.

Scheier, M. F., and C. S. Carver. 1993. On the power of positive thinking: The benefits of being optimistic. *Current Directions in Psychological Science* 2 (1): 26–30.

Seligman, M. E. P. 1991. *Learned Optimism.* New York: Alfred A. Knopf & Sons.

Seligman, M. E. P., K. Reivich, L. Jaycox, and J. Gillham. 1995. *The Optimistic Child.* Boston: Houghton Mifflin.

Snyder, C. R. 1994. *The Psychology of Hope: You Can Get There from Here*. New York: Free Press.

Taylor, S. E. 1989. *Positive Illusions: Creative Self-Deception and the Healthy Mind*. New York: Basic Books.

Wegner, D. M. 1989. *White Bears and Other Unwanted Thoughts: Suppression, Obsession, and the Psychology of Mental Control*. New York: Penguin Books.

These are the sources for the claims about research findings and reviews of theoretical arguments that I make throughout the book:

CHAPTER 1

Peterson, C., and L. M. Bossio. 1991. *Health and Optimism*. New York: Free Press.

Scheier, M. F., and C. S. Carver. 1993. On the power of positive thinking: The benefits of being optimistic. *Current Directions in Psychological Science* 2 (1): 26–30.

Sheldon, K. M., and L. King, eds. 2001. Positive psychology. Special section, *American Psychologist* 56: 216–249.

Taylor, S. E. 1989. *Positive Illusions: Creative Self-Deception and the Healthy Mind*. New York: Basic Books.

CHAPTER 2

Chang, E. C. 1998. Distinguishing between optimism and pessimism: A second look at the optimism-neuroticism hypothesis. In *Viewing Psychology as a Whole: The Integrative Science of William N. Dember,* ed. R. R. Hoffman, pp. 415–432. Washington, D.C.: American Psychological Association.

Cohen, F., K. A. Kearney, L. S. Zegans, M. E. Kemeny, J. M. Neuhaus, and D. P. Stites. 1999. Differential immune system changes with acute and persistent stress for optimists vs. pessimists. *Brain, Behavior, and Immunity* 13 (2): 155–174.

Dember, W. N., S. H. Martin, M. K. Hummer, and S. R. Howe. 1989. The measurement of optimism and pessimism. *Current Psychology: Research and Reviews* 8 (2): 102–119.

Marshall, G. N., C. B. Wortman, J. W. Kusulas, and L. K. Hervig. 1992. Distinguishing optimism from pessimism: Relations to fundamental dimensions of mood and personality. *Journal of Personality and Social Psychology* 62 (6): 1067–1074.

Norem, J. K. 1989. Cognitive strategies as personality: Effectiveness, specificity, flexibility, and change. In *Personality Psychology: Recent Trends and Emerging Directions,* ed. D. M. Buss and N. Cantor, pp. 45–60. New York: Springer-Verlag.

Peterson, C. 1995. Explanatory style and health. In *Explanatory Style,* ed. G. M. Buchanan, pp. 233–246. Hillsdale, N.J.: Lawrence Erlbaum Associates.

Plomin, R., M. F. Scheier, C. S. Bergeman, and N. L. Pedersen. 1992. Optimism, pessimism, and mental health: A twin/adoption analysis. *Personality and Individual Differences* 13 (8): 921–930.

Raeikkoenen, K., K. A. Matthews, J. D. Flory, J. F. Owens, and B. B. Gump. 1999. Effects of optimism, pessimism, and trait anxiety on ambulatory blood pressure and mood during everyday life. *Journal of Personality and Social Psychology* 76 (1): 104–113.

Scheier, M. F., and C. S. Carver. 1985. Optimism, coping, and health: Assessment and implications of generalized outcome expectancies. *Health Psychology* 4 (3): 219–247.

References

Schulman, P., D. Keith, and M. E. Seligman. 1993. Is optimism heritable? A study of twins. *Behaviour Research and Therapy* 31 (6): 569–574.

Seligman, M. E. P. 1991. *Learned Optimism*. New York: Alfred A. Knopf & Sons.

Seligman, M. E. P., K. Reivich, L. Jaycox, and J. Gillham. 1995. *The Optimistic Child*. Boston: Houghton Mifflin.

Weinstein, N. D. 1980. Unrealistic optimism about future life events. *Journal of Personality and Social Psychology* 39 (5): 806–820.

CHAPTER 3

Barlow, D. H. 1996. Fear, panic, anxiety, and disorders of emotion. In *Nebraska Symposium on Motivation, 1995: Perspectives on Anxiety, Panic, and Fear,* ed. D. A. Hope, pp. 251–328. Lincoln: University of Nebraska Press.

Dweck, C. S. 1986. Motivational processes affecting learning. *American Psychologist* 41 (10): 1040–1048.

Elliot, A. J., and H. A. McGregor. 1999. Test anxiety and the hierarchical model of approach and avoidance achievement motivation. *Journal of Personality and Social Psychology* 76 (4): 628–644.

Fyer, A. J. 1993. Heritability of social anxiety: A brief review. *Journal of Clinical Psychiatry* 54 (12, Suppl.): 10–12.

Knowles, J. A., S. Mannuzza, and A. J. Fyer. 1995. Heritability of social anxiety. In *Social Phobia: Clinical and Research Perspectives,* ed. M. B. Stein, pp. 147–161. Washington, D.C.: American Psychiatric Press.

Norem, J. K., and N. Cantor. 1990. Cognitive strategies, coping, and perceptions of competence. In *Competence Considered,* ed. R. J.

Sternberg and J. Kolligian, Jr., pp. 190–204. New Haven: Yale University Press.

Pyszczynski, T., and J. Greenberg. 1987. Self-regulatory perseveration and the depressive self-focusing style: A self-awareness theory of reactive depression. *Psychological Bulletin* 102 (1): 122–138.

Stein, M. B., ed. 1995. *Social Phobia: Clinical and Research Perspectives.* Washington, D.C.: American Psychiatric Press.

Thapar, A., and P. McGuffin. 1995. Are anxiety symptoms in childhood heritable? *Journal of Child Psychology and Psychiatry and Allied Disciplines* 36 (3): 439–447.

Van Dijk, W. W., and J. van der Plight. 1997. The impact of probability of outcome on disappointment and elation. *Organizational Behavior and Human Decision Processes* 69: 227–284.

CHAPTER 4

Illingworth, K. S. S. 1993. *Cognitive Strategies and Mood: The Role of Affect in the Strategic Use of Optimism and Defensive Pessimism.* Unpublished doctoral dissertation, Northeastern University, Boston.

Norem, J. K., and N. Cantor. 1986. Defensive pessimism: Harnessing anxiety as motivation. *Journal of Personality and Social Psychology* 51 (6): 1208–1217.

Norem, J. K., and N. Cantor. 1986. Anticipatory and post hoc cushioning strategies: Optimism and defensive pessimism in "risky" situations. *Cognitive Therapy and Research* 10 (3): 347–362.

Norem, J. K., and K. S. S. Illingworth. 1993. Strategy-dependent effects of reflecting on self and tasks: Some implications of optimism and defensive pessimism. *Journal of Personality and Social Psychology* 65 (4): 822–835.

Norem, J. K., and K. S. S. Illingworth. 2001. Mood Effects Depend on Personality: Performance among Strategic Optimists and Defensive Pessimists. Unpublished manuscript.

Sanna, L. J. 1996. Defensive pessimism, optimism, and stimulating alternatives: Some ups and downs of prefactual and counterfactual thinking. *Journal of Personality and Social Psychology* 71 (5): 1020–1036.

Sanna, L. J. 1998. Defensive pessimism and optimism: The bittersweet influence of mood on performance and prefactual and counterfactual thinking. *Cognition and Emotion* 12 (5): 635–665.

Spencer, S. M. 1993. *Defensive Pessimism and Strategic Optimism in the Athletic Domain: An Evaluation of Performance Outcomes and Health-Related Aspects.* Unpublished doctoral dissertation, Northeastern University, Boston.

Spencer, S. M., and J. K. Norem. 1996. Reflection and distraction: Defensive pessimism, strategic optimism, and performance. *Personality and Social Psychology Bulletin* 22 (4): 354–365.

CHAPTER 5

Arkin, R. M., K. C. Oelson, K. G. Shaver, and D. J. Schneider. 1998. Self-handicapping. In *Attribution and Social Interaction: The Legacy of Edward E. Jones,* ed. J. M. Darley, pp. 313–371. Washington, D.C.: American Psychological Association Press.

Campbell, J. D., P. D. Trapnell, S. J. Heine, I. M. Katz, L. F. Lavallee, and D. R. Lehman. 1996. Self-concept clarity: Measurement, personality correlates, and cultural boundaries. *Journal of Personality and Social Psychology* 70 (1): 141–156.

Cheek, J. M., and A. H. Buss. 1981. Shyness and sociability. *Journal of Personality and Social Psychology* 41 (2): 330–339.

Elliot, A. J., and K. M. Sheldon. 1998. Avoidance, personal goals, and the personality-illness relationship. *Journal of Personality and Social Psychology* 75 (5): 1282–1299.

Eronen, S., J. E. Nurmi, and K. Salmela Aro. 1998. Optimistic, defensive-pessimistic, impulsive, and self-handicapping strategies in university environments. *Learning and Instruction* 8 (2): 159–177.

Gaertner, L., C. Sedikides, and K. Graetz. 1999. In search of self-definition: Motivational primacy of the individual self, motivational primacy of the collective self, or contextual primacy? *Journal of Personality and Social Psychology* 76 (1): 5–18.

Harris, R. N., C. R. Snyder, R. L. Higgins, and J. L. Schrag. 1986. Enhancing the prediction of self-handicapping. *Journal of Personality and Social Psychology* 51 (6): 1191–1199.

Jones, E. E. 1976. How do people perceive the causes of behavior? *American Scientist* 64: 300–305.

Jones, E. E., and S. Berglas. 1978. Control of the attributions about the self through self-handicapping strategies: The appeal of alcohol and the role of underachievement. *Personality and Social Psychology Bulletin* 4: 200-206.

Kelley, H. H. 1973. The process of causal attribution. *American Psychologist* 28: 107–128.

Leary, M. R., and J. A. Shepperd. 1986. Behavioral self-handicaps versus self-reported handicaps: A conceptual note. *Journal of Personality and Social Psychology* 51 (6): 1265–1268.

Martin, A. J., H. W. Marsh, and R. L. Debus. 2001. Self-handicapping and defensive pessimism: Exploring a model of predictors and outcomes from a self-protection perspective. *Journal of Educational Psychology* 93 (1): 87–102.

References

Numazaki, M. 1995. Effects of acquired and claimed self-handicapping on receivers' impressions. *Japanese Journal of Experimental Social Psychology* 35 (1): 14–22.

Pelham, B. W. 1991. On confidence and consequence: The certainty and importance of self-knowledge. *Journal of Personality and Social Psychology* 60 (4): 518–530.

Rhodewalt, F., D. M. Sanbonmatsu, B. Tschanz, and D. L. Feick. 1995. Self-handicapping and interpersonal trade-offs: The effects of claimed self-handicaps on observers' performance evaluations and feedback. *Personality and Social Psychology Bulletin* 21 (10): 1042–1050.

Robins, R. W., J. K. Norem, and J. K. Cheek. 1999. Naturalizing the self. In *Handbook of Personality,* 2nd ed., ed. L. A. Pervin, pp. 443–477. New York: Guilford Press.

Tice, D. M. 1991. Esteem protection or enhancement? Self-handicapping motives and attributions differ by trait self-esteem. *Journal of Personality and Social Psychology* 60 (5): 711–725.

CHAPTER 6

Block, J., and C. R. Colvin. 1994. Positive illusions and well-being revisited: Separating fiction from fact. *Psychological Bulletin* 116 (1): 28.

Cantor, N., and J. K. Norem. 1989. Defensive pessimism and stress and coping. *Social Cognition* 7 (2): 92–112.

Cantor, N., J. K. Norem, C. Langston, and S. Zirkel. 1991. Life tasks and daily life experience. *Journal of Personality* 59 (3): 425–451.

Cantor, N., J. K. Norem, P. M. Niedenthal, C. A. Langston, and A. M. Brower. 1987. Life tasks, self-concept ideals, and cognitive strategies in a life transition. *Journal of Personality and Social Psychology* 53 (6): 1178–1191.

Carver, C. S., C. Pozo, S. D. Harris, and V. Noriega. 1993. How coping mediates the effect of optimism on distress: A study of women with early stage breast cancer. *Journal of Personality and Social Psychology* 65 (2): 375–390.

Carver, C. S., S. K. Sutton, and M. F. Scheier. 2000. Action, emotion, and personality: Emerging conceptual integration. *Personality and Social Psychology Bulletin* 26 (6): 741–751.

Colvin, C. R., and J. Block. 1994. Do positive illusions foster mental health? An examination of the Taylor and Brown formulation. *Psychological Bulletin* 116 (1): 3–20.

Colvin, C. R., J. Block, and D. C. Funder. 1995. Overly positive self-evaluations and personality: Negative implications for mental health. *Journal of Personality and Social Psychology* 68 (6): 1152–1162.

Davidson, K., and K. Prkachin. 1997. Optimism and unrealistic optimism have an interacting impact on health-promoting behavior and knowledge changes. *Personality and Social Psychology Bulletin* 23 (6): 617–625.

Goldfried, M. R. 1979. Anxiety reduction through cognitive-behavioral intervention. In *Cognitive-Behavioral Interventions: Theory, Research, and Practice,* ed. C. K. S. D. Hollon. New York: Academic Press.

Kiehl, E. 1994. *Attitudes Towards AIDS Among Unrealistic Optimists, Health Optimists, and Health Defensive Pessimists.* Unpublished Honors Thesis, Wellesley College, Wellesley, Mass.

Lyubomirsky, S., K. L. Tucker, N. D. Caldwell, and K. Berg. 1999. Why ruminators are poor problem solvers: Clues from the phe-

References

225

nomenology of dysphoric rumination. *Journal of Personality and Social Psychology* 77 (5): 1041–1060.

Meichenbaum, D. 1977. *Cognitive Behavior Modification: An Integrated Approach.* New York: Plenum Press.

Norem, J. K. 1988. Strategic realities: Optimism and defense pessimism. *Dissertation Abstracts International* 48 (11-B): 3444–3445.

Norem, J. K. 1998. Why should we lower our defenses about defense mechanisms? *Journal of Personality* 66 (6): 895–917.

Norem, J. K. 2000. Defensive pessimism, optimism, and pessimism. In *Optimism and Pessimism: Implications for Theory, Research, and Practice,* ed. E. C. Chang, pp. 77–100. Washington, D.C.: American Psychological Association Press.

Norem, J. K., and N. Cantor. 1990. Capturing the "flavor" of behavior: Cognition, affect, and interpretation. In *Affect and Social Behavior,* ed. B. S. Moore, pp. 39–63. New York: Cambridge University Press; Paris: Editions de la Maison des Sciences de L'Homme.

Norem, J. K., and E. C. Chang. 2000. A very full glass: Adding complexity to our thinking about the implications and applications of optimism and pessimism research. In *Optimism and Pessimism: Implications for Theory, Research, and Practice,* ed. E. C. Chang, pp. 347–367. Washington, D.C.: American Psychological Association Press.

Park, C. L., P. J. Moore, R. A. Turner, and N. E. Adler. 1997. The roles of constructive thinking and optimism in psychological and behavioral adjustment during pregnancy. *Journal of Personality and Social Psychology* 73 (3): 584–592.

Showers, C. 1992. The motivational and emotional consequences of considering positive or negative possibilities for an upcoming event. *Journal of Personality and Social Psychology* 63 (3): 474–484.

Showers, C., and C. Ruben. 1990. Distinguishing defensive pessimism from depression: Negative expectations and positive coping mechanisms. *Cognitive Therapy and Research* 14 (4): 385–399.

Snyder, C. R. 1994. *The Psychology of Hope: You Can Get There from Here*. New York: Free Press.

Stein, M. B., K. L. Jang, and W. J. Livesley. 1999. Heritability of anxiety sensitivity: A twin study. *American Journal of Psychiatry* 156 (2): 246–251.

Taylor, S. E., and J. D. Brown. 1988. Illusion and well-being: A social psychological perspective on mental health. *Psychological Bulletin* 103 (2): 193–210.

Tennen, H., and G. Affleck. 1987. The costs and benefits of optimistic explanations and dispositional optimism. *Journal of Personality* 55 (2): 377–393.

van der Pligt, J., W. Otten, R. Richard, and F. van der Velde. 1993. Perceived risk of AIDS: Unrealistic optimism and self-protective action. In *The Social Psychology of HIV Infection,* ed. J. B. Pryor, pp. 39–58. Hillsdale, N.J.: Lawrence Erlbaum Associates.

Weinstein, N. D. 1982. Unrealistic optimism about susceptibility to health problems. *Journal of Behavioral Medicine* 5 (4): 441–460.

Weinstein, N. D., and E. Lachendro. 1982. Egocentrism as a source of unrealistic optimism. *Personality and Social Psychology Bulletin* 8 (2): 195–200.

CHAPTER 7

Bless, H., G. L. Clore, N. Schwarz, and V. Golisano. 1996. Mood and the use of scripts: Does a happy mood really lead to mindlessness? *Journal of Personality and Social Psychology* 71 (4): 665–679.

Carver, C. S., L. A. Kus, and M. F. Scheier. 1994. Effects of good versus bad mood and optimistic versus pessimistic outlook on social acceptance versus rejection. *Journal of Social and Clinical Psychology* 13 (2): 138–151.

Derryberry, D., and M. A. Reed. 1994. Temperament and attention: Orienting toward and away from positive and negative signals. *Journal of Personality and Social Psychology* 66 (6): 1128–1139.

Dewberry, C., M. Ing, S. James, and M. Nixon. 1990. Anxiety and unrealistic optimism. *Journal of Social Psychology* 130 (2): 151–156.

Diener, E. 2000. Subjective well-being: The science of happiness and a proposal for a national index. *American Psychologist* 55 (1): 34–43.

Eisenberg, N., R. A. Fabes, I. K. Guthrie, and M. Reiser. 2000. Dispositional emotionality and regulation: Their role in predicting quality of social functioning. *Journal of Personality and Social Psychology* 78 (1): 136–157.

Gilbert, D. T., and J. G. Hixon. 1991. The trouble of thinking: Activation and application of stereotypic beliefs. *Journal of Personality and Social Psychology* 60 (4): 509–517.

Green, D. P., P. Salovey, and K. M. Truax. 1999. Static, dynamic, and causative bipolarity of affect. *Journal of Personality and Social Psychology* 76 (5): 856–867.

Rothbart, M. K., S. A. Ahadi, and D. E. Evans. 2000. Temperament and personality: Origins and outcomes. *Journal of Personality and Social Psychology* 78 (1): 122–135.

Sanna, L. J., K. J. Turley, and M. M. Mark. 1996. Expected evaluation, goals, and performance: Mood as input. *Personality and Social Psychology Bulletin* 22 (4): 323–335.

Schwarz, N., and G. L. Clore. 1983. Mood, misattribution, and judgments of well-being: Informative and directive functions of affective states. *Journal of Personality and Social Psychology* 45 (3): 513–523.

Sedikides, C. 1992. Mood as a determinant of attentional focus. *Cognition and Emotion* 6 (2): 129–148.

Vosberg, S. K. 1998. Mood and the quality and quantity of ideas. *Creativity Research Journal* 11: 315–331.

Wenzlaff, R. M., D. M. Wegner, and S. B. Klein. 1991. The role of thought suppression in the bonding of thought and mood. *Journal of Personality and Social Psychology* 60 (4): 500–508.

CHAPTER 8

Aspinwall, L. G., and S. E. Taylor. 1993. Effects of social comparison direction, threat, and self-esteem on affect, self-evaluation, and expected success. *Journal of Personality and Social Psychology* 64 (5): 708–722.

Blanton, H., J. Crocker, and D. T. Miller. 2000. The effects of ingroup versus out-group social comparison on self-esteem in the context of a negative stereotype. *Journal of Experimental Social Psychology* 36 (5): 519–530.

Bushman, B. J., and R. F. Baumeister. 1998. Threatened egotism, narcissism, self-esteem, and direct and displaced aggression: Does self-love or self-hate lead to violence? *Journal of Personality and Social Psychology* 75 (1): 219–229.

Chang, E. C. 1996a. Cultural differences in optimism, pessimism, and coping: Predictors of subsequent adjustment in Asian American and Caucasian American college students. *Journal of Counseling Psychology* 43 (1): 113–123.

Chang, E. C. 1996b. Evidence for the cultural specificity of pessimism in Asians vs. Caucasians: A test of a general negativity hypothesis. *Personality and Individual Differences* 21 (5): 819–822.

Chemers, M. M., C. B. Watson, and S. T. May. 2000. Dispositional affect and leadership effectiveness: A comparison of self-esteem, optimism, and efficacy. *Personality and Social Psychology Bulletin* 26 (3): 267–277.

Cramer, P. 1995. Identity, narcissism, and defense mechanisms in late adolescence. *Journal of Research in Personality* 29 (3): 341–361.

Gibbons, F. X., and M. Gerrard. 1989. Effects of upward and downward social comparison on mood states. *Journal of Social and Clinical Psychology* 8 (1): 14–31.

Heine, S. J., T. Takata, and D. R. Lehman. 2000. Beyond self-presentation: Evidence for self-criticism among Japanese. *Personality and Social Psychology Bulletin* 26 (1): 71–78.

Hickman, S. E., P. J. Watson, and R. J. Morris. 1996. Optimism, pessimism, and the complexity of narcissism. *Personality and Individual Differences* 20 (4): 521–525.

Holtgraves, T., and R. Hall. 1995. Repressors: What do they repress and how do they repress it? *Journal of Research in Personality* 29 (3): 306–317.

Kernis, M. H., and C. R. Sun. 1994. Narcissism and reactions to interpersonal feedback. *Journal of Research in Personality* 28 (1): 4–13.

Kruger, J., and D. Dunning. 1999. Unskilled and unaware of it: How difficulties in recognizing one's own incompetence lead to inflated self-assessments. *Journal of Personality and Social Psychology* 77 (6): 1121–1134.

Petrie, K. J., R. J. Booth, and J. W. Pennebaker. 1998. The immuno-
logical effects of thought suppression. *Journal of Personality and
Social Psychology* 75 (5): 1264–1272.

Reis, H. T., K. M. Sheldon, S. L. Gable, J. Roscoe, and R. M. Ryan.
2000. Daily well-being: The role of autonomy, competence, and
relatedness. *Personality and Social Psychology Bulletin* 26 (4):
419–435.

Rudich, E. A., and R. R. Vallacher. 1999. To belong or to self-
enhance? Motivational bases for choosing interaction partners.
Personality and Social Psychology Bulletin 25 (11): 1387–1404.

Rudman, L. A., and P. Glick. 1999. Feminized management and
backlash toward agentic women: The hidden costs to women of a
kinder, gentler image of middle managers. *Journal of Personality
and Social Psychology* 77 (5): 1004–1010.

Wunderley, L. J., W. B. Reddy, and W. N. Dember. 1998. Optimism
and pessimism in business leaders. *Journal of Applied Social
Psychology* 28: 751–760.

CHAPTER 9

Dalziel, J. R., and R. F. S. Job. 1997. Motor vehicle accidents, fa-
tigue, and optimism bias in taxi drivers. *Accident Analysis and
Prevention* 29 (4): 489–494.

Paulhus, D. L., P. D. Trapnell, and D. Chen. 1999. Birth order effects
on personality and achievement within families. *Psychological
Science* 10 (6): 482–488.

Reppucci, J. D., T. A. Revenson, M. Aber, and N. D. Reppucci. 1991.
Unrealistic optimism among adolescent smokers and nonsmok-
ers. *Journal of Primary Prevention* 11 (3): 227–236.

Shanahan, M. J., F. J. Sulloway, and S. M. Hofer. 2000. Change and constancy in developmental contexts. *International Journal of Behavioral Development* 24 (4): 421–427.

Sulloway, F. J. 1996. *Born to Rebel: Birth Order, Family Dynamics, and Creative Lives*. New York: Pantheon Books.

Taylor, S. E., and R. M. Gollwitzer. 1995. The effects of mindset on positive illusions. *Journal of Personality and Social Psychology* 69: 213–226.

Taylor, S. E., M. E. Kemeny, L. G. Aspinwall, S. G. Schneider, R. Rodriguez, and M. Herbert. 1992. Optimism, coping, psychological distress, and high-risk sexual behavior among men at risk for acquired immunodeficiency syndrome (AIDS). *Journal of Personality and Social Psychology* 63: 460–473.

Tennen, H., and G. Affleck. 1998. Personality and transformation in the face of adversity. In *Posttraumatic Growth: Positive Changes in the Aftermath of Crisis,* ed. R. G. Tedeschi, pp. 65–98. Mahwah, N.J.: Lawrence Erlbaum Associates.

More information about defensive pessimism can be found on the Internet at www.defensivepessimism.com

Acknowledgments

I could write a book about all the help and support I've received writing this book, but I'll try to control myself. Nancy Cantor has been a wonderfully generous mentor; she started the program of research on defensive pessimism. Quite literally, this book would not exist without her. Darrin Lehman and Carolin Showers were instrumental in the development of the early descriptions of the strategy, and Carolin Showers has done a substantial portion of the systematic research on defensive pessimism.

My eternal gratitude goes to my colleagues over the years, especially Lisa Feldman Barrett, Chris Langston, Bill Fleeson, Steve Harkins, Rob Sellars, Carolin Showers, Elissa Wurf, and Sabrina Zirkel, who have listened to me think out loud long after most people would have nodded off to sleep. I also owe much to William Dember, Edward C. Chang, and Lawrence Sanna, whose work has renewed my inspiration. Ed's energetic pursuit of a well-rounded perspective on optimism and pessimism has reaffirmed my conviction that defensive pessimism is a worthwhile topic. Past and present students have also provided invaluable help conducting this research and otherwise clarifying my thinking. Special thanks to collaborators Shaun Illingworth, Stacie Spencer-Perna, Eliza McCardle, and Sonia Worcel. Regan Bernhard, Amy Gower, Shannon Smith, and the students from my seminar on optimism and pessimism have all provided humor, help, insight, and encouragement throughout the writing process.

Patricia Byrne, Blythe Clinchy, Gale Empey, David Pillemer, Jane Pillemer, and Diana Chapman Walsh all generously gave of their time and acumen, and I am grateful for their help. Elizabeth Knoll, Tim Bartlett, and David Pillemer made me believe both that people might be interested in defensive pessimism and that I might be able to write a book. Cindy Hyden, editor-cum-therapist and friend, gave unstintingly of her effort, experience, and wisdom, as she helped the seeds of this book grow into a much more judiciously pruned yet robust product than what I could have produced without her (for which readers, too, should be grateful). I'm also indebted to Jo Ann Miller, executive editor at Basic Books, for the leap of faith and powerful advocacy that allowed an actual book to appear after mere conversations, to Jessica Callaway, her editorial assistant, for her gentle reminders throughout the process, and to Wesley Weisberg for the analogy with which I end the book.

The Positive Power of Negative Thinking

My family—parents, brother, aunts, uncles, cousins, and in-laws—has always been my ultimate resource and refuge, as they were again while I wrote this book. Nikki Schall, Aaron Kopf, Amy Gower, Megan Kross, Stella Kakavouli, Takis Metaxas (all of whom are really family, too), and the phenomenal teachers at WCCC keep my life from falling apart. To my son, Nathan, an accomplished author at age eight, for his empathetic concern throughout the writing process; to my daughter, Haley, for the two-year-old's exuberance that is the world's best diversion; and to my husband, Jonathan Cheek, for his confidence that this could happen, his insight and experience as a psychologist, and the support that helped me along, all my gratitude and all of my love.

Acknowledgments

Index

The Positive Power of Negative Thinking

Index

About the Author

J ulie K. Norem, Ph.D., is Associate Professor of Psychology at Wellesley College. She has published many articles on personality and social behavior in psychology journals. Her work on defensive pessimism has been cited in *The New York Times*, *SELF*, the *Washington Post*, *Men's Health*, *McCall's*, and *American Health*, and she maintains her own Web site, www.defensivepessimism.com. She lives in Wellesley, MA.